AF642101

Edited by Johanna Domokos, Johanna Laakso

Multilingualism and multiculturalism in Finno-Ugric Literatures 2

Finno-Ugrian Studies in Austria

Schriftenreihe für die Forschungsbereiche
der Abteilung Finno-Ugristik
(Institut für Europäische und
Vergleichende
Sprach- und Literaturwissenschaft)
an der Universität Wien

herausgegeben von
Andrea Seidler
Johanna Laakso

Band 9

LIT

Multilingualism and multiculturalism in Finno-Ugric Literatures 2

Edited by
Johanna Domokos
Johanna Laakso

LIT

Peer reviewed by Naomi Caffee, Vuokko Hirvonen,
Lore Knapp, Michal Kovář, Levente Seláf,
Antje Wischmann
Language editing by Catharina Krallmann,
Georgina Willms
Design by Gergely Lőrincz

Bibliographic information published by the Deutsche Nationalbibliothek
The Deutsche Nationalbibliothek lists this publication in the Deutsche Nationalbibliografie; detailed bibliographic data are available on the Internet at http://dnb.d-nb.de

978-3-643-91001-1 (pb)
978-3-643-96001-6 (PDF)

A catalogue record for this book is available from the British Library

© LIT VERLAG GMBH & CO. KG WIEN
Zweigniederlassung Zürich 2020
Flössergasse 10
CH-8001 Zürich
Tel. +41 (0) 44-251 75 05
E-Mail: zuerich@lit-verlag.ch
www.lit-verlag.ch

Distribution:
In the UK:
Global Book Marketing
E-mail: mo@centralbooks.com

In North America:
Independent Publishers Group
E-mail: orders@ipgbook.com

In Germany:
LIT Verlag Fresnostr. 2, D-48159 Münster
Tel. +49 (0) 2 51-620 32 22, Fax +49 (0) 2 51-922 60 99
E-mail: vertrieb@lit-verlag.de

E-books are available at www.litwebshop.de

Contents

7 Introduction: Finno-Ugric Literatures and Multilingualism

15 Multicultural Dialogue in László Végel's Neoplanta, avagy az Ígéret Földje — Erika Bence

39 Multilingualism in the contemporary Finnish literature (Suomen kirjallisuus) — Johanna Domokos

61 Hungarian Migrant Writers in the West since 1945 — Károly Kókai

75 Multilingualism in Finno-Ugric Minority Literatures: Authenticity vs. Emancipation? — Johanna Laakso

107 The Voice Crying (or Calling?) in the Wilderness. Possible Similarities between Transylvanism and Meänmaa-Idea — Enikő Molnár Bodrogi

129 On the History of Translation into Udmurt — Vera Grigorievna Panteleeva

147 The Allegorisation of Minority Space in Slovakian Hungarian Literature — Anikó Polgár

163 Writing in the Dominant Language — Eva Toulouze

181 List of contributors

Introduction – Finno-Ugric literatures and Multilingualism Studies

The Editors

One of the central tasks of comparative literary studies is to define and promote world literature as well as developing the necessary critical tools for its comparative analysis. This requires a form of detached engagement with all literature, and all kinds of literary worlds besides the national literatures and canons promoted in academia or by today's book market. As we understand world literature along with David Damrosh (2003), as a mode of production, circulation, and reading of literary works, this publication draws attention to the multilingual and multicultural history and corpus of individual Finno-Ugric/Uralic literatures. Just as the Finno-Ugric literatures, most literatures of the world can only exist as multicultural practices. Most of them are minoritarian literatures that live in prescriptive linguistic cultures and their language planning is influenced by traditionally monolingual and puristic ideals of the dominant national languages as an "ideal code". However, at the same time, minority literatures may have an emancipatory agenda which implies realistic description of language-related issues, including code-switching and code-mixing.

Literature as an exemplificatory medium of art and culture enjoys high prestige among all Uralic peoples. Even though they rely on fictional worlds, their literatures offer valuable insights into relevant issues of their often multilingual everyday life. These literary fields contain a vast amount of information about the performativity of cultures in highly multicultural and transcultural settings, as well as local, regional, and global aspects of power practices and ecological and ecocultural issues (just to mention some of the many possibilities). Since most of the Uralic languages (in fact all, except the three nation-state languages, Estonian, Finnish, and Hungarian, in their respective states) are endangered or highly endangered, the ecology of their literatures and cultures is also highly endangered. The creative usage of the language leading to literary works contributes enormously to keeping a linguistic community in their traditional communication.

The term "Finno-Ugric/Uralic literatures" has been constructed on the basis of linguistic relatedness. Although this relatedness is fairly distant (far beyond mutual intelligibility or visible resemblance in almost all cases, with the exception of a few subgroups of sister varieties), it has played a symbolic role in the national or ethnic emancipation of many Uralic-speaking peoples and accordingly, in the genesis of their literary cultures. However, this term covers a diversity of historical situations and language-political positions. Today, this literary "Finno-Ugritude" seems to be enlivened and performed mostly by minority literatures from the north of Scandinavia to West Siberia in the eastern colonization zone of historical Russia. The literatures of the Uralic-speaking state nations – Estonia, Finland, and Hungary – are based on more strongly established national traditions, and their literary agents are less inclined to incorporate a minoritarian paradigm. Even the literatures of minority and diaspora groups using these three major languages, such as the literatures of the traditionally Hungarian-speaking areas outside today's Hungary (see chapters 1, 5, and 7) or the literature of the Finnish migrants in Sweden, typically align with the national paradigms rather than to the position of other Finno-Ugric minorities. It is important to realize that the concept of Finno-Ugric literatures is the product of comparative literary theories and interests, not historical relationships. The tradition of Finno-Ugric/Uralic literature research rests on existing research practices, human networking (e.g. meetings, conferences, and cultural festivals of Uralic peoples), and the distribution of literary translations.

This volume offers an insight into multilingual literary practices in a broad range of literatures, positioned in different sociopolitical contexts. The westernmost Finno-Ugric literatures are written in the sociocultural frameworks of European nation-states, by majorities or minorities in different settings, from the young Saami, Kven, and Meänkieli literatures in the Far North to the literary traditions of Hungary and the Hungarian minorities in Central Europe. In Russia, two main types of Uralic literatures exist.. The Mordvin, Mari, Udmurt, and Komi peoples in European Russia have titular republics with various institutions to support the ethnic language and its literature; nevertheless, despite six-figure speaker numbers and a literary tradition with a history of often more than a hundred years, these languages are endangered. The Finnic and easternmost Saami languages in the Northwest of European Russia as well as the Uralic languages of Siberia, viz. the Ob-Ugric (Khanty and Mansi) and Samoyed languages, with speaker numbers ranging from tens of thousands (Karelian in the Finnic group, Nenets in the Samoyedic group) to just a handful, typically have less - established literary traditions, and some of these languages are hardly used in writing. Despite their vastly different socio-ecological environments, the Finno-Ugric minority literatures of Russia have all been either created or at least strongly formed by the ethnopolitics of the Soviet Union, de facto continued in the Russian Federation, and the literacy practices of these peoples are marked by the models of Russian literature and the prescriptive Russian linguistic culture.

The articles of this volume are based on papers presented at our symposium “Finno-Ugric literary multilingualism and multiculturalism" at the 12th Congress of Finno-Ugric Studies in Oulu (Finland) in 2015. The symposium was the second one of its kind; the first symposium on this topic was organized by the same researchers in 2010 at the 11th Congress of Finno-Ugric Studies in Piliscsaba (Hungary). The present publication aims to follow the same goals as the preceding publication entitled "Multilingualism and Multiculturalism in the Uralic literatures" (2011), and emphasises the need of further research in this area. Studies on literary multilingualism involving minority languages often focus on the presence of minority languages in majority-language literature. They mostly investigate how minority language elements challenge the reader or "make silenced voices heard". Therefore, this publication wishes to turn the focus of research around and so examines literatures written mostly in (Finno-Ugric) minority languages and the presence of dominant languages in their literary contexts. However, investigations of multilingual practices of Finno-Ugric literatures with national status (Finnish, Hungarian and Estonian) are also well represented in this book.

In the first chapter entitled "Multicultural Dialogue in László Végel's Neoplanta, avagy az Ígéret Földje" Erika Bence examines the linguistic and cultural codes of the two narrators who have different ethnic identities. László Végel, a Hungarian author from the province of Vojvodina/Vajdaság in Serbia, places the story of this 2014 novel in the city of Újvidék (in Serbian: Novi Sad), the capital of Vojvodina. The two narrators of the novel, the author-narrator and Lazo Pavletić the coach-driver, while driving along the streets of the city, tell and re-tell, from their own perspectives and in their own languages, the 20th-century history of Újvidék and its geographic environment, that is, Vojvodina. The discourse between the Hungarian author and the Serbian coachman forms, necessarily, a multilingual and multicultural dialogue, given that the city from its founding on has been home to a diversity of linguistic and cultural otherness of its ethnic groups (Hungarians, Serbs, Germans, Slovaks, Jews, and others), different habituses and collective memories. Paradoxically enough, although the city was founded in the spirit of peaceful coexistence, throughout the centuries these groups have continuously oppressed and murdered each other. In times of crises, wars and power shifts, they have stood on opposite sides, yet the catastrophes and cul-de-sacs they have experienced have been the same or of a similar character.

Chapter two – Johanna Domokos's study on "Code-switching in Suomen kirjallisuus/ Finnish literature – reports on the growing importance of multilingualism/code-switching in Finnish literature. This study argues that code-switching is a constitutive act for contemporary literature in Finland, where it repeals linguistic and cultural barriers, de-automizes semantic production, addresses the appropriation of linguistic, aesthetic and cultural diversity, and stages alterity. Reflections on literary code-switching with regard to grammatical structure, aesthetic production, and socio-cultural significance result in the differentiation of five code-switching techniques applicable not only to Finnish literature, but to other traditions as well. These numerated degrees, defined on the basis of Myers-Scotton's concepts of intra- and inter-sentential code-switching, matrix language, and embedded language (1993), allow for the mapping of an entire spectrum of literary code-switching from its covert to overt manifestations.

Károly Kókai's study on "Hungarian Migrant Writers in the West since 1945" concentrates on the works of emigrated Hungarian writers in German, French, English, and Italian cultural environments, characterized by conflicts of both languages and cultures. Some prominent examples include Sándor Márai, György Sebestyén, and Agota Kristof. Márai, despite his German roots (his family name was originally Grosschmid) and his multicultural background in the city of Kassa/Košice in today's Slovakia, wrote his major works in Hungarian. He migrated via Italy to the USA after World War II. Sebestyén, who left Hungary for Austria in 1956, published his first book in the West in Hungarian and was an editor of a Hungarian language daily in Vienna for several years before switching to the German language and becoming, in his own words, an "Austrian writer". Kristof, also a 1956 emigrant, lived in Switzerland and wrote in French. The paper argues for a differentiated look, allowing for an understanding of the host cultures by way of the cultural productions of migrants; for a definition of culture including minorities and migrants; and for applying scientific tools developed in postcolonial studies to discuss the oeuvres of migrant writers, using the examples of Márai, Sebestyén and Kristof.

Modern minorities are multilingual, and the presence of the dominant language (or other languages as well, such as Lingua Franca English) characterizes their everyday lives. However, many minorities live in prescriptive linguistic cultures, and their language planning is influenced by traditionally monolingual and puristic ideals of the national language as an "ideal code". In chapter four, Johanna Laakso's study on "Multilingualism in Finno-Ugric Minority Literatures: Authenticity vs. Emancipation?" concentrates on minority literatures that have an emancipatory agenda, which implies realistic description of language-related issues, including code-switching and code-mixing. Contrary to studies on literary multilingualism focusing on the presence of minority languages in majority-language literature, this chapter concentrates on literatures written in Finno-Ugric minority languages and on questions of authenticity and emancipation. It reflects beyond the realistic representation of real-life multilingualism on the question of what other functions can the presence of other languages in the text have, and what are the linguistic and poetic dimensions along which these can or should be investigated.

The comparative study by Enikő Molnár Bodrogi entitled as "The Voice Crying (or Calling?) in the Wilderness: Possible Similarities between Transylvanism and Meänmaa-Idea" in chapter five focuses on two Finno-Ugric minorities, the Hungarians in Romania and the Meänkieli-speaking Tornedalians in Sweden, from the perspective of two possibly analogous ideologies, and examines their influence upon the aesthetic and literary self-identifying program of their representatives. There are, obviously, many differences between Transylvanism (the ideology of ethnic consciousness of Hungarians in Transylvania harmonized with cultural pluralism) and the idea of Meänmaa 'Our Country' (the trans-border region of the Meänkieli speakers on the Swedish side and the speakers of originally the same dialect on the Finnish side of the border), since there are also differences in the histories of the Hungarians in Transylvania and the Meänkieli-speaking Tornedalians. By looking to the literary production of the pioneers of these two ideologies, of Károly Kós and Bengt Pohjanen, this study concentrates on the possible similarities between the two systems of ideas and their impact on the literature of these minorities. It analyses topics such as the interpretations of minority existence, traumas of the history and strategies of processing them, the bidirectional act of constructing and deconstructing borders, and the symbolic value of one's minority mother tongue in the context of an intolerant society of the majority language.

Chapter six turns our focus to the Udmurt literary field active in Central Russia. In her contribution "On the History of Translation into Udmurt", Vera Grigorievna Panteleeva deals with the characteristics of each of the five periods of the history of translation into Udmurt with a focus on the principles, functions and aesthetic significance of the translated works.

In chapter seven, Anikó Polgár's "The Allegorisation of Minority Space in Slovakian Hungarian Literature" discusses the relationship between space and identity in the context of Hungarian literature in Slovakia, based on the concept of multiculturalism and minor(ity) literature. It claims that it is not necessary to strictly differentiate between works that directly reflect on the Hungarian surroundings in Slovakia and those that are of a more universal relevance. In an allegorical sense, the latter can also refer to the problems of identity arising from the dwindling of minority space or the superimposition of different elements. To illustrate this point, the author analyses the storybooks entitled Tamarindusz (Tamarind) and Alacindruska, demonstrating that tales also include, on an allegorical level, the multiculturalism of the minority space as well as its attitudes to diversity.

The closing chapter eight by Eva Toulouze entitled "Writing in the Dominant Language" examines the language choices of Finno-Ugric authors. We have been accustomed to thinking about language as the primary ethnic marker and thus we automatically connect national/ethnic literatures with the national/ethnic language. However, this is not always the case, even with national literatures of nation states, and even less so with minority literatures such as the Finno-Ugric literatures in Russia. The first part of this chapter discusses the language-based identity of Finno-Ugric writers at the beginning of the ethnic literarisation projects, and analyses those literary works written in Russian that may be categorised as belonging to the ethnic literatures. The second part of the study concentrates on more recent examples of how authors affiliated to the Finno-Ugric peoples of Russia use the Russian language. The chapter concludes with analysing the Russian-language works of authors of the Mansi and Nenets peoples in the Russian Far North.

With this volume, we wish to give the reader a glimpse of the diversity of Uralic literatures and the numerous aspects of multilingualism and multiculturalism present in these literatures in countless ways – in nation-states with multilingual and multiethnic traditions, in minority literatures struggling with the challenges of endangerment, revitalization and identity construction, and in migrant literatures as well as nation-state literatures reacting to new forms of migration and multiculturalism. We are happy and grateful to all authors for their inspiring contributions and ideas. Our warmest thanks are also due to all of the peer revievers and the language editors of the text.

Bielefeld and Vienna, March 15, 2018

Multicultural dialogue in László Végel's Neoplanta, avagy az Ígéret Földje

Erika Bence

Translated by Johanna Laakso

1. Introduction

The existence of different histories and the otherness of cultural memories, in the sense of Hayden White (1973) and Jan Assmann (1988), can be recognized in the narratives which constitute László Végel's novel *Neoplanta, avagy az Ígéret Földje* ('Neoplanta, or the Promised Land', Végel 2013). The virtual protagonist of this prose work, which calls itself an "urban novel" (Toldi 2010; Roginer 2015), is Újvidék (Novi Sad), the capital of the province of Vojvodina, and its history is told by two narrators of different identities, different linguistic and culturalaffiliations[1] (Assmann 1988; Assmann 1992; Assmann and Czaplicka 1995), as seen through their own linguistic or cultural codes and their communally legitimized historical memories (Ankersmit 1989). One of them, the Serbian coachman Lazo Pavletić, is the son of a soldier who in World War I deserted from the Austrian army to the Serbian side and thus marched (or rode)

1. "Das kulturelle Gedächtnis hat seine Fixpunkte, sein Horizont wandert nicht mit dem fortschreitenden Gegenwartspunkt mit. Diese Fixpunkte sind schicksalhafte Ereignisse der Vergangenheit, deren Erinnerung durch kulturelle Formung (Texte, Riten, Denkmäler) und institutionalisierte Kommunikation (Rezitation, Begehung, Betrachtung) wachgehalten wird" (Assmann 1988, 12).

into the city in the ranks of the victorious army, and a woman whose ethnic affiliation, Slovak or Hungarian, remains unclear: she was called Katarina Horáková or Horák Katalin, for some time she was even forced to call herself Katarina Horaković.[2] The other narrator is the Hungarian author from the Hungarian-speaking settlement of Szenttamás who in 1956, accompanied by his father, arrives in the city on bicycle, to continue his studies in a Hungarian-language secondary school and to live in a student dormitory among students of diverse ethnic groups coming from all over Yugoslavia – here, he represents an ethnic minority. For both narrators, the city forms the locus of cultural contacts and conflicts, a history of continuous shifts of linguistic and cultural identities.

2. The inhabitants of Újvidék and the whole region have in the course of power shifts and reorganization of state structures often been forced to change their identities, languages, and names.

According to a popular story, Újvidék was founded in the spirit of multiculturality, as emphasized by the Empress Maria Theresia in the founding decree, originally in Latin:

> *Its name shall be Neoplanta, and each people shall give it a name in their own language. Let them live in peace, love each other, and let this city of many peoples be an example of the peaceful coexistence of different nations.*
> (Végel 2013, cover text)

Meanwhile, the history of 250 years since then has witnessed the opposite of this: "since then, its peoples have continuously murdered each other" (Végel 2013, cover text).

2. Narratives of irony and anecdote

Partly continuing the traditions of the genesis of Hungarian literature, partly expressing the irony of the narratability or un-narratability of history, László Végel's urban history is built on anecdotes, the anecdote in itself representing a technique to cover lies and untruths (Gallop 2002):

> *The anecdote as a genre has been present in our literature for centuries, practically untouched by those transforming or transsubstantiating processes which have systematically deplaced other forms*

and types of speech or made them antiquated, old-fashioned, unsuitable. It is present in the Hungarian prose of the late 20th or the early 21st century in the same way as it was in the novels and short stories of the second half of the 19th century. The explanation to this – presumably – lies in its special quality of being not just a category of language or a genre but a form of existence in itself, an understanding of the world which is essentially based on memories and untruths.
(Bence 2008, 76)

In this sense, it is in discourse with more than a century-old traditions of novel-writing[3] (for instance, the novels of Kálmán Mikszáth). In his foreword to the novel *Beszterce ostroma* ('The Siege of Beszterce', 1894), Mikszáth describes the relation of the anecdote as the basis of a novel to societal forms: in this novel, this societal form is represented by a merry fellowship at table (Bence 2015b). In Végel's novel, the context for story-telling is provided by coach-rides in the city. Throughout decades, Pavletić the coachman and the author drive in gallop through the streets of Újvidék while telling stories about the same thing, the history of the city, stories about essentially the same thing (there are many histories of the same past), only from different perspectives. The difference lies not in the language (both are fluent in each other's language, Serbian or Hungarian) but in the cultural codes. The same history, the reflection of the great history in the fates of different peoples, is shown either from the point of view of the Serbian majority, historically based on the position of the Serbian armed forces which marched as victors into the city in 1918 (one of the cavalry regiments was led by Major Lazo Pavletić Sr., the coachman's father), or from the perspective of the author, coming from the ethnic group which was autochthonous and "state-forming" in the Austro-Hungarian empire but lost the World Wars and turned into a minority in the former Southern provinces.

Végel's novel reflects and reproduces the anecdotal story-telling mode of the turn of the 20th century also in the sense that the conversation partners (as in Mikszáth's texts) are situated both inside and outside the story.

3. See Dobos 1995; Eisemann 1998.

The language of the story is peculiar: the meanings of its codes and symbols only reveal themselves to those positioned inside the story, to those who know this particular language (of untruths). Lazo Pavletić tells a lot, many short stories and anecdotes from World War II and the Communist era which followed it, but he is not willing and not even able (his death puts an end to this) to discover the truth hidden under the chain of anecdotes. The author gradually acquires the insider code of the anecdotes, learns to know the truth which is hidden behind the stories and unfolded in their interconnections, and this helps him especially in understanding his own and his generation's identity and revealing the untruths connected to it. Throughout his life, Lazo Pavletić carries the truth in himself, surrounding it with diverse stories, concealing and lengthening the road to the point where the truth is openly told, and dies when arriving at the end of this road. The author in turn (presumably, due to the different coding of his generation-specific and cultural background) uses irony and self-revealing conclusions to relieve the historical and cultural tensions which are due to the fact that in this region and its history, a person can simultaneously be a hero and a traitor, good and bad, in the same way as an historical narrative is simultaneously true and untrue. A striking example of this is provided by Lazo Pavletić himself and his story, or rather an anecdote told by the author. This anecdote tells about a photo in the city museum, showing Tito's partisans marching into the city, and of this photo – as well as of the story itself, the story of Miklós Török – there exists also an earlier, hidden version.

The novel is a series of anecdotes told many times, from many points of view (in the voice of the coachman, the author, and also in a neutral narrator's voice in the background) and in many versions. From behind these anecdotes, by way of details, causes and consequences which can gradually be conjectured from a network of coincidences, the truth is slowly unfolded. In the stories of Lazo Pavletić, a recurring figure is Döme Bujdosó, a man dressed in a white shirt, white trousers and a shepherd's white sheepskin coat, clutching a Bible in his hand and preaching about the "yellow danger" and the end of the world. With him, Pavletić will sit in the bar of the

Csillag hotel in endless conversations, at other times, he threatens Bujdosó with his gun, demanding him to kneel down and ask for forgiveness.

The narrator has known them for years before he finally discovers the background of their strange friendship: both have a dark secret to hide, and both know each other's secret. Döme Bujdosó, who used to dress in white and serve as a cemetery guard during World War II, once "changed his clothes" to a grey suit when marrying Hilda Brunner, the pretty and cheeky widow of an SS officer who had fallen in Bosnia. Hilda was of Swabian (local German) extraction, but changing her name and identity with the new marriage and meeting the arriving partisans with a bouquet of flowers did not save her: one night she disappeared. Rumours had it that she had charmed the partisans as well and been taken to Belgrad, where she became the lover of a Serbian general or even Marshall Tito himself. More probably, however, she ended up in one of the nameless graves in the cemetery, betrayed by her own husband who dug her grave with his own hands. Lazo Pavletić probably knows this, while Bujdosó, now again a humble cemetery guard in his white clothes, spreads the gossip that Pavletić, in order to prove his loyalty to the partisans, had himself executed his friends.

As for the latter claim, there are some details indicating that it might be true or at least close to truth. After World War II, with the partisans seizing power, Lazo Pavletić – presumably, driven by his premonitions or pangs of conscience – invites his best friends and war-time front companions, the Hungarian János Novák and the German Ottó Oswald, for dinner. Both arrive in white, ironed shirts and black trousers. This will be – as Lazo Pavletić calls it, decades later – their "last supper". At the same night, Pavletić's friends are seized and they end up in the unmarked mass grave of the Catholic cemetery. It is not excluded, although never proven (the only witness is Döme Bujdosó, not quite reliable either), that they were betrayed by Lazo Pavletić himself. The gesture of "the last supper" (Pavletić may have been assigned this task, or maybe he just sensed that his friends were in danger but failed to warn them) and other signs show that the coachman suffers from a guilty conscience until the end of his life. After the disappearance of his friends, he takes care of their houses, horses and carriages, while knowing or at least sensing that they are no more alive. On one occasion, he even visits their mothers, bringing sweets and chocolate (which in the after-war years count as a luxury). Finally, the coachman's last words before his death can be understood as referring to the fate of his friends:

> *Ezek szerint lehet az ember hős is, meg gyáva is, egy személyben. Húsz évvel ezelőtt még abban hittem, hogy az ember vagy hős, vagy gyáva. Legalábbis, normál körülmények között, így lenne rendjén. Viszont ebben a városban minden összekuszálódott. Egyszerre hős és gyáva. Gyilkos és áldozat. Ha életben marad, akkor bizonyára nem lesz belőle hős, hanem alávaló, gyáva kukac... Gyalázatos. Így kell megdögleni, így kell lemosni a szégyent, a kurva úristenit ennek a világnak...*
>
> 'This shows that one can be a hero and a coward in one person. Twenty years ago I still believed that a man is either a hero or a coward. At least under normal circumstances it would be normal. But in this city everything got messed up. Hero and coward at the same time. Murderer and victim. If you survive, you certainly won't become a hero but a base, cowardly maggot... It's shameful. This is how one must die, this is how one must wash away the shame, goddamn this fucking world...'
> (Végel 2013, 26) (my translation)

"This shows" in Lazo's last words refers to an anecdote which plays an essential role in the novel. The hero of the anecdote, Miklós Török, was a contemporary of the author's. Together, they carried the Youth Relay Baton in one of the most important symbolic events of the Titoist dictatorship. Miklós Török's father had during the so-called "cold days", the raids of 1942, protected and hidden his neighbour who later became known as Comrade Ivanka Jovanović, although he didn't share her ideological conviction. In 1944, during the revenge actions of the partisans, Ivanka Jovanović could have saved

Török's life but failed to intervene in time. Because of this, until the end of her life – probably driven by remorse – she supported her neighbour's son, Miklós Török Jr., in his life and career. Miklós Török Jr. is perhaps the only character in *Neoplanta* who is able to face his own and his family's crimes, cowardice and treason. This leads to a moral breakdown, and he chooses to put an end to his life in a strange way: being a doctor, he doesn't accept any treatment for his disease. He also utters the weightiest words in the narrator's stories (Bence 2015a):

> *Ebben a városban kétféle ember létezik, az egyik beleszületik a bűnbe, a másik meggyőződésből vállalja. Néha alig van különbség a kettő között. [...] Sohasem tudjuk, hogy melyik csoportba tartozunk, lehet, hogy mindkettőbe. Nincs értelme ettől menekülni, bűnhődnünk kell. Valakiért, valamiért, teljesen mindegy.*
>
> 'In this city, there are two kinds of people, some are born in crime, others accept it out of conviction. Sometimes, there is almost no difference between these two. [...] We never know which group we belong to, perhaps to both of them. It's no use running away from this, we must suffer for our sins. For somebody, for something, it makes no difference at all.'
> (Végel 2013, 257)

In an intertextual sense, László Végel's *Neoplanta, avagy az Ígéret Földje* is closely connected to the novel *Ez a nap a miénk* ('This day belongs to us', 1997 [2007]) by Nándor Gion (1941–2002), another author hailing from Szenttamás. The latter novel also consists of narratives around the shifts of power in the same region, the tragicomedy of forces "marching in and out", in it as well tragic anecdotes are told about how the helpless inhabitants of the region fell victim to revenge acts with diverse ideological and cultural backgrounds. And while *Neoplanta* is part of a trilogy (*Bűnhődés* 'Atonement', 2012; *Neoplanta, avagy az Ígéret Földje*, 2013; *Balkáni szépség avagy Slemil fattyúja* 'Balkan beauty, or Shlemiel's bastard', 2015), the novel *Ez a nap a miénk* belongs to a tetralogy (*Virágos Katona* 'Soldier with flowers', 1973; *Rózsaméz* 'Rose honey', 1976; *Ez a nap a miénk*, 1997; *Aranyat talált* 'He found gold', 2002 [2007]).

2.1 The ritual of marching in and the discreet charm of leaving

As mentioned above, the father of Lazo Pavletić, a Serbian soldier from Croatia conscripted to the Austrian army in World War I, had deserted to the Serbian side. With his bravery he advanced to a major's rank, and in 1918 he, leading a cavalry regiment, rode into the city of Újvidék, which he saw as the Promised Land:

> *Délcegen ült a nyeregben, nem tudott betelni a rendezett város látványával, megigézték a gyönyörű, elegáns hölgyek, akik csókjaikat hintették a bevonuló katonai menetoszlop felé, az ízlésesen öltözött úriemberek, akik egyik kezükben sajtóterméket szorongattak, a másik kezükben sétabotot tartottak.*
>
> 'Sitting gallantly in the saddle, he could not get enough of watching this beautifully organized city, he was fascinated by the lovely, elegant ladies throwing kisses towards the marching columns of soldiers, by the tastefully dressed gentlemen who held some printed matter in their one hand and a walking stick in the other.'
> (Végel 2013, 44)

In the eyes of Lazo Pavletić Sr. – at that time, still a young bachelor – it is especially the clothing that makes the local people distinct, completely different from his own people. He has no knowledge of the traditions, memories and distinctions of cultural identity (Assmann 1988). For this reason, "he, too, wanted to be like them" (Végel 2013, 45), and in order to achieve this, he "changes clothes", putting on the suit of the Hungarian officer whose former house he has occupied, and performs a ritual of purification, which in his case means "completing his toilet".

> *Olyan érzés vett erőt rajta, mintha újjászületett volna. Ettől kezdve minden áldott nap*

> *kiillatosítva, ünneplőben hagyta el a házat. Már ébredezett benne a vágy, hogy igazi újvidéki lakos legyen. Olyan úriemberré vedlik, mint a kisasszonyokat kísérgető gavallérok. Megmutatja milyen átalakulásra képes!*
>
> 'He was overwhelmed by the sensation of being reborn. From that day on, every single day he left the house perfumed, in his best attire. He was already starting to wish that he might become a real Újvidék man. Be a gentleman like those who escort young ladies. Show how he can transform himself!'
> (Végel 2013, 59)

Lazo Pavletić Jr. – by an irony of fate, as the narrator states – "he, the son, was in 1941 at the same place watching the whole parade of the arriving Hungarian army" (Végel 2013, 265). To his surprise, his sick old father, the "liberator" of yore, already experienced in these matters, comments on the events:

> *Nyugodj bele, fiam, boldog-boldogtalan meghódította már ezt a várost. Ne törődj vele! Nekünk, fiákereseknek csak az a fontos, hogy az urak tisztességesen viselkedjenek a bérkocsiban. És ne sokat lövöldözzenek.*
>
> 'Accept this, my son, this city has already been occupied by everybody. Don't care! For us coachmen, the only important thing is that the gentlemen will behave themselves while sitting in our cab. And not shoot around too much.'
> (Végel 2013, 266)

When arriving in this Promised Land, as Újvidék seems to be or is shown, each new power stages a strange parade. The ritual is the same, often with the same participants, only in different situations and affiliations. This is illustrated by the story of the father of Miklós Török, who was seen on the same balcony twice, witnessing the parade of two different occupying forces, and – allegedly – photographed in both situations. The first photo was kept well hidden by the family. In it, Miklós Török's father is celebrating the arrival of the Hungarian army in a "Bocskai [Hungarian national-romantic pseudo-military] overcoat, in the second line, standing with raised arms behind the speaker" (Végel 2013, 251). The second photograph is shown in the city museum:

> *[...] azon szintén a nagyapa látható. A második sorban ugyanazon az erkélyen görnyedten ácsorog. A szónok magasba emelt karral üdvözli a bevonuló partizánokat. Mögötte a nagyapa, homlokára tolt, vászonból készült partizánsapkával a fején amelyen ötágú vörös csillag díszelgett.*
>
> '[...] on it, as well, the grandfather is seen. He is in the second line on the same balcony, standing stooped. The speaker, with his arms raised, is greeting the partisans who march in. Behind him the grandfather, with a partisan cap made of canvas pushed down on his forehead, on it shone the five-pointed red star.'
> (Végel 2013, 251)

When the armed men of this latter power came to get him, old Török "dressed carefully", despite the commander raging at him "that he shouldn't play for time, he won't escape anyway." (Végel 2013, 256) Similar sarcastic comments are voiced by the henchmen in *Ez a nap a miénk.* One of them, for instance, says to Rojtos Gallai: "You can dig your grave in a white shirt as well. True, the white shirt will get dirty, but under the earth nobody will see it." (Gion 2007, 631)

2.2 The culture of "getting dressed" – anecdotes of code-switching

The story-teller Lazo Pavletić always wears a black suit and a bowler hat; he also attaches a great importance to correct clothing and corresponding behaviour. Through this, he also measures and evaluates the changes in the cultural situation of the city:

> *A vasárnap délutáni sétakocsikázást szerettem leginkább, amikor az utasokat a Csillag*

Szállodától hazáig szállítottam. [...] Ünnepi fuvarok voltak. Ők voltak az utolsó újvidéki úriemberek, akiknek dukált, nem utolsósorban imponált, hogy a vasárnapi családi ebéd után fiákerrel kocsikázzanak haza. Tudtak élni, megadták a módját. Ilyen kuncsaftból mára egyre kevesebb maradt, mert sajnos, kihalnak a régi újvidékiek. Vég nélkül jönnek az újak, a régiek pedig azon keseregnek, hogy kivesznek az őslakók, miközben senki sem hajlandó tudomásul venni, hogy mindnyájan jöttmentek vagyunk.

'What I used to like best were the rides on Sunday afternoons, when I took passengers home from the Csillag hotel. [...] Those were festive rides. They were the last gentlemen of Újvidék who thought it fitting or even impressive to ride home from a Sunday family lunch in a cab. They knew how to live, they knew how to spend. Today, there are fewer and fewer such customers, because, sadly enough, traditional Újvidék people are dying out. New people keep coming, while the old ones are complaining how the old inhabitants of the city are dying out, while nobody cares to realize that all of us are newcomers.'
(Végel 2013, 27)

The 20th-century history of Újvidék is, by nature, characterized by shifts of powers and ideologies. Each new power, as a rule, arrives with a great hullabaloo, murders those who belong to the opposite camp (ethnic or religious community) or who have different convictions, and leaves with full-loaded lorries. This is how the Serbian Mrs Grgić describes it to the Slovak mother of Lazo Pavletić:

Nem lesz többé itt Sacher-torta sem, meg illatos, forró csokoládé sem. Bele kell törődnöd. Mi, akarom mondani, a szerbek felszabadultak, viszont meglásd, ezek a kommunisták úgy kifosztanak bennünket, hogy ihaj! Nekünk nincs póthazánk, nincs hova elinalnunk. A magyar urak megpakolt teherautókkal hordták el az irhájukat. Vitték a szajrét: a stílbútorokat, az ékszereket, a drága

> *bundákat, a porcelánszervizeket, az étkészleteket, az ezüsttálcákat meg az evőeszközöket, a kristályt, a damasztágyneműt, de még a matracokat is. Mondd, hova, merre húzza a csíkot az én férjem? Hova meneküljön egy igazi szerb úriember? A mi értékeinket nem menti meg senki.*
>
> 'There will be no more Sacher cakes here, nor that aromatic hot chocolate. You'll have to live with it. We, I mean, the Serbs were liberated, but you'll see, these Communists will rob us bare! We don't have a spare homeland, we have nowhere to go. The Hungarian gentlemen saved their skins and escaped in loaded lorries. They took their things: the period furniture, the jewelry, the expensive fur coats, the porcelain tableware, the silver platters and knives and forks, the crystal glasses, the damask bed linen, even the mattresses. Tell me, where can my husband go? Where should a real Serbian gentleman escape? Nobody will save our valuables.' (Végel 2013, 67–68)

The same "argument" is used by the narrator (in the stories of Lazo and the author), from a superior, ironical point of view, in the case of Miss Meinert who was humiliated by the Russians:

> *Szép is, csinos is, burzsuj is, örüljön, hogy élve maradt, ha már cserbenhagyták a szerencsétlent a magyar urak, akik 1914-ben diadalmasan harsogták, hogy nem, nem soha. Aztán haptákba vágták magukat az újvidéki magyar hölgyek előtt, és esküdöztek, hogy visszajönnek. Kezét csókolom, nagyságos asszony, mondták, majd jól megtömték szajréval a teherautót. Vitték az ékszereket, az étkészleteket, a stílbútorokat, a szőrmebundákat. Mentették az irhájukat.*
>
> 'She is beautiful, and pretty, and bourgeois as well, she should be happy to have survived, once she, poor thing, was let down by the Hungarian gentlemen who in 1914 triumphantly trumpeted "no, no, never" [= a slogan connected

with Hungarian irredentism]. They saluted the Hungarian ladies of Újvidék and swore that they would return. Kiss your hand, my lady, they said, then packing the lorries with things. They took the jewelry, the tableware, the period furniture, the fur coats. They saved their skins.'
(Végel 2013, 90)

The "changing clothes" and "washing oneself" after bloody acts of revenge is also one of the topics in Nándor Gion's novel *Aranyat talált* ('He found gold', 2002), the fourth book in a tetralogy:

> *A szerb partizánok levetették egyenruhájukat, hősködni hősködtek még, de már nem lehetett büntetlenül gyilkolni a németeket és a magyarokat, megszűntek a mészárlások, a maradék németeket kitelepítették, ők a későbbiekben igen jól jártak, a magyarokat nem ritkították tovább, nagyjából helyrerázódott a nyugalom a Délvidéken, tehát Szenttamáson is. A kiürített német házakba lomha, sokgyerekes hegyi lakókat költöztettek be. A jövevények tanácstalanul tévelyegtek a síkságon, nehezen illeszkedtek be a környezetbe.*
>
> 'The Serbian partisans took off their uniforms, they were still playing heroes, but it was no more allowed to murder Germans and Hungarians unpunished, the butchering ended, the remaining Germans were deported, later on they were really lucky, Hungarians were not decimated any further, for the most part the Southern provinces, including Szenttamás, were wrenched back into a state of peace. Into the emptied German houses, sullen people from the mountains, with many children, were accommodated. The newcomers wandered around on the plain, clueless, it was difficult for them to acclimatize.'
> (Gion 2007, 720)

In the late 1960s, Tito's Socialist Yugoslavia opens up its borders, which results in a change of populations and in particular forms of migration. On the one hand, masses of *Gastarbeiter* move to Germany, returning home every summer with Western cars packed full of things, while a certain shadow of suspicion surrounds them: certainly some of them have been "recruited by the German secret police" (Végel 2013, 105). On the other hand, the banished Germans return to visit their old homes, alarming the "colonists", the newcomers who have been settled in their places and provoking the fear in them that "the Swabians who return in masses will get their houses, fields, and factories back." (Végel 2013, 105). This, of course, is an unfounded rumour, after long years of peace arousing the illegitimate usurpers' fears, while for the Germans, these visits to their former homelands rather mean something like coming to terms with their conscience:

> *Mintha ezzel is meg akarták volna vásárolni az itteniek jóindulatát, szerették volna megnyugtatni saját lelkiismeretüket. Heimat, Heimat, mondogatták megilletődve. Batschka und Banat. Poharazgatás közben néha kiszaladt a szájukon, hogy Hitler a főbűnös, és hál' isten, nekik semmi közük hozzá. A kolonisták gyanakodva figyelték a jövevényeket, miközben azt puhatolták, hogy mit jelent az a szó, hogy Heimat. Szülőföld, világosították fel őket gyermekeik. Pa, šta? I mi smo izgubili svoju domovinu. Joj, naša predivan Bosna, ili ti božanstvena Crna Gora, to je naša prava domovina. Obećali nam je da ćemo jesti zlatnim kašikama, međutim od toga nema ništa. A Švabe stižu.*
>
> 'As if by this as well they would have wanted to buy the goodwill of the local people, to pacify their own conscience. *Heimat, Heimat,* they repeated in awe. *Batschka und Banat.* Between the glasses of wine, sometimes it slipped out of their mouth that Hitler was the main bad guy and thank God, they had nothing to do with him. The colonists watched the newcomers suspiciously while trying to find out what the word *Heimat* meant. Homeland, their children informed them. *Pa, šta?* [starting from here, the words of the Yugoslav newcomers are given in Serbo-Croatian] So what? We have also lost our homeland. Oh, our lovely Bosnia,

or you, the divine Montenegro, that's our true homeland. They promised us that we would be eating with golden spoons here, but nothing has come out of it. But the Krauts are coming back.' (Végel 2013, 106)

Into the bipolar flow of the story, a narrator regularly interferes from above, with ironical comments. The Western tourists and visitors boarding Lazo Pavletić's cab – for their sake, the coachman even studies English – are shown in an ironically distorted perspective, in the same way as those who "escaped in time" and now return to visit their former homes. The former ones are visiting these Southern regions, escorted with state pomp, so that they might say: in contrast to the false Western democracy, how original is the primeval force of the Balkans! Yet, they are striving to get back to their velvet Western democracies which they themselves have sentenced to death. (Végel 2013, 239)

As for the latter ones:

> *Késztetést érez, hogy hébe-hóba visszatérjen a pátriát meg nemzetét magasztalni, tanújelét adva a szülőföld iránti hűségnek. Úgy tesz, mint aki nem tudja, hogy érzelmi kitörése, rajongása jól begyakorolt alakoskodás része. Nem meri kimondani azt, amit gondol, hogy ezt a várost barbárok lakják, akik meg akarják hódítani az Ígéret Földjét.*
>
> 'They feel an urge to rush back, to praise their fatherland and nation, to testify of their loyalty towards their homeland. They pretend not to know that their emotional outbursts, their devotion is part of well-trained simulation. They don't dare to say what they think: that this city is inhabited by barbarians who want to conquer the Promised Land.'
> (Végel 2013, 239)

Both Végel's novel and the novels by Gion mentioned here as a parallel example are impregnated with a fatalist faith, the hope that in the end, the guilty ones will meet Nemesis. In *Ez a nap a miénk,* Anđelina Simin, the former collaborator of a partisan killer squad, is found on a summer morning in fishermen's net in the river; how she got there is never found out, but most people believe that the people from Ság killed her, revenge formurder of their brother Imre. In *Neoplanta,* the fate of Miklós Török is the best illustration of how the forces of fate form the life and death of an individual. His father is first executed and then posthumously honoured as a war hero by the same Communist power. It turns out that the father of his wife in those times presided at the summary court that gave the death sentence. At the funeral of his son-in-law, the cynical murderer breaks down, kneels, and starts praying to God for forgiveness. Even more tragically, some ordinary people such as the father and, especially, the son Pavletić, had to commit crimes unwillingly or even against their will. In the 1970s, Katarina Horáková meets Miss Meinert again, who was not crushed by the tragic events; on the contrary, she has made an academic career in Germany. However, she still feels extremely embarrassed for what happened – by being an eye-witness, even against her will, she has in some way turned into a participant of the collective violence which has shaped today's world.

2.3 Ball and orgy in the coffee-house: the Dornstädter anecdote

The centre of the actions is *Szabadság tér,* the Freedom Square, which the author-narrator also calles the Big Lie Square, the place where the Pavletić coachmen waited for their customers throughout decades and where – as if to the Promised Land – Pavletić senior in his time rode in with his Serbian regiment. On the same square, the crowds waited for the partisans, here rolled the tanks of the Hungarian army, here throughout the postwar decades the Baton Relay of Tito was hailed, and here, of course, was the scene of the mass demonstrations in connection with the most recent sudden conversions: "where we now are screaming at the top of our lungs that we never ever wanted to go that way." (Végel 2014, 22).

On Freedom Square, there is the Dornstädter coffee house, which in the course of its history functions under many names; the changes in regular customers, portraits of heads of state on the wall, and the name of the establishment itself reflect the changes of ideologies and party positions. Before 1918, the portrait of Franz Josef I hung on the wall and officers of the imperial army treated young ladies with cakes and hot chocolate. After World War I, Serbian officers filled the coffee house and the city authorities gave an order to hang the portrait of King Peter on the wall, and in 1941, when the coffee house became the favourite meeting place of Hungarian officers, the most conspicuous place of the hall had to be decorated with a portrait of Regent Horthy. According to the narrator(s), Mr Dornstädter – had he been able – would obviously have put the portraits of Tito and Stalin as well on the wall, since according to his conviction, it wasn't important

> *kinek a képe csüng a falon, meg vendégeink egyenruhája, [...] hanem a Sacher torta íze meg a kávé illata, illetve a nálunk kapható finomság originalitása. [...] Mellékes, hogy milyen nyelven rendel a vendég, vagy hogy milyen ancúgban van, az a fontos, hogy rendeljen és fizessen. A pénznek nincs szaga!*
>
> 'whose picture is hanging on the wall, or the uniforms of our customers, [...] it's the taste of the Sacher cake and the aroma of coffee, or the originality of the delicacies available here. [...] It's irrelevant in what language the customer places his orders or what kind of suit he is wearing, the important thing is that he orders and pays. Money doesn't stink!'
> (Végel 2014, 66)

However, the portraits of Stalin and Tito are not put on the wall by Mr Dornstädter, who disappears after the war, but by the henchman of the new Communist power, the head waiter Šuković. Only the mother of Lazo Pavletić, Katalin Horák of unclear extraction (Slovak? Hungarian?), a former waitress of the coffee house, still hopes that Mr Dornstädter, who appreciated the quality and dignity of service more than anything else, could have escaped somehow.

In this coffee house, symbolic of the whole city of Újvidék, important social events take place, such as the carnival balls, which also provide the locus for the expression of each current ideology. In 1940, when the

German-born Miss Meinert is elected as the queen of the ball, the madness of the war is already swiftly spreading. As the father of the ball queen, the owner of a soap factory, gives an anti-war speech, he is not met with the usual fervent applause.

> *[...] Olyasmit talált mondani, hogy nem lenne jó, ha itt is öldöklésbe torkolna a viszály. Meg hogy Újvidéket valamiképp meg kellene kímélni. Nem engedhetjük meg, hogy csorbuljon a szabad királyi város tekintélye."*
>
> '[...] what he thought appropriate to say was something like that it would not be good if here as well the conflicts would lead to people killing each other. And that Újvidék should somehow be spared. We cannot allow the prestige of the free royal city to be diminished.'
> (Végel 2013, 87)

In 1941, the crowd of course toasts a Hungarian ball queen, who

> *könnybelábadt szemekkel rebegte, hogy amíg szüleivel budapesti száműzetésben gyászolta Trianont, minduntalan nyomasztotta a gondolat, hogy szegény délvidéki magyarok mennyit kénytelenek nélkülözni. Egyebek mellett a finom magyar pezsgőt is nélkülözik.*
>
> 'stuttered with tears in her eyes that, while she with her parents in her Budapest exile was mourning Trianon [= the peace treaty of 1920 which detached these regions as well from Hungary], she had all the time been depressed by the thought of what the poor Hungarians in the Southern provinces were missing. Among other things, they also had to miss the fine Hungarian sparkling wine.'
> (Végel 2013, 88)

She, of course, is one of the first to leave Újvidék after the lost war, while the refined and educated Miss Meinert stays, claiming that she has not committed any crimes. This is what she repeats while Russian soldiers, in front of the crowd watching through the windows with perverted glee, rape her in the Dornstädter coffee house, now renamed "Moscow". The cultural change following the power shift is described in a characteristic way by Katalin Horák, the mother of Lazo Pavletić, who also witnesses the shameful deed at the Dornstädter coffee house and is the only one to feel shame for it until the end of her life: "[...] when did the lace curtains turn yellowish, why are the plush armchairs squeaking, why is the parquet so dirty?" (Végel 2013, 78).

2.4 The Danube as a symbol of the lie

Dictators of all times present themselves to the masses – misled or prejudiced, or, rather, reduced to rabble – most often wearing the mask of the "wise father". The bourgeoisie of Újvidék, for example, saw their saviour in either Hitler or Horthy, depending on their ethnic affiliation. Miklós Horthy was hailed on the main square of Újvidék in 1942 with the same script and the same rhetorics as Marshall Tito in 1944. The Serbian Marić with his entourage departs for Serbia in a lorry full of belongings in the same way as the Horthyist gentlemen leave for Hungary – their servants, in turn, remain in their roles of helpless little people, such as Katarina Horáková/Horák Katalin, or the old Mrs. Novák.

The armed forces of the shifting powers first enjoy the celebrations with brutal demagogy on the Trinity/Freedom/Big Lies Square, then shoot members of another nation or ethnic group into the Danube which flows nearby. Because of this, the author-narrator attempts in his festival speeches to demystify this false picture and subtopos of the Danube as "the blue ribbon of Europe":

> *„A bérkocsiból rémülten bámultam Európa legnagyobb folyóját, a sötét, rideg, nagyméretű tömegsírt. Yes, yes, ismételgettem magamban, a Duna összeköt bennünket. Ezt hajtogattam, holott utólag beláttam, itt kellett volna fennhangon folytatnom a mondatot. Yes, massgrave. Kimondani, szembesülni a szavak erejével. Large mass grave in the Danube. Massengrabe. Viele*

grosse Massengraben in der Donau, die Deutcshen, sebs, magyarok, zsidók, yes, Jews, Juden, Jevreji, ja, ja, együtt élünk a tömegsírokkal, hogyisne, hiszen a limesen szent hevülettel gyilkoljuk egymást; csak hát erről bölcsen hallgatunk.

'From the cab, I watched in terror the greatest river of Europe, that dark, cold, massive mass grave. *Yes, yes,* I repeated to myself, the Danube connects us. This is what I kept repeating, although afterwards I realized that I should have continued the sentence aloud. *Yes, massgrave.* To say it out loud, to face the force of the words. *Large mass grave in the Danube. Massengrabe. Viele große Massengraben in der Donau, die Deutschen, Serbs,* Hungarians, Jews, *yes, Jews, Juden, Jevreji, ja, ja,* we live together with the mass graves, of course, here at the *limes* we murder each other in holy fervour; it's just that we wisely keep silent about that.'
(Végel 2013, 237).

The city of Neoplanta–Újvidék–Neusatz–Novi Sad has continuously been liberated throughout its 250 years of existence. In the early 1990s, the novel author once dreams that the city is being liberated once again, and among the celebrating crowd he again meets the already deceased Miklós Török, who explains his stance (being a doctor, he did not allow his disease to be treated) by telling that "he didn't want to be ordered to stand on any balcony any more", which is why he "escaped – to death" (Végel 2013, 264). The narrator in his dream runs in panic away from the celebrations on the Freedom Square, rushes to a place on the Danube shore called the "Square of Crimes", and there, raising his arm, he throws the relay baton into the Danube, the blood-stained mass grave.

3. Conclusion: two anecdotes as the opportunity of covering up lies and as a way to multicultural understanding

The 20th-century history of Újvidék in László Végel's novel *Neoplanta, avagy az Ígéret Földje* is composed of a series of anecdotes, each based on blood-stained stories. One of the great anecdotes is connected to Comrade

Tito's visit in Újvidék. The author-narrator – in the same way as readers beyond a certain age – is, in accordance with the character of the anecdote, simultaneously a participant of this story and its recipient. As a student in Újvidék, he is present in the crowd which has been commanded to meet Tito, shouting hurrah and claiming with conviction (like many others) that the Marshall has waved to him to, especially to him. In his student years, he also learns to know the "great narrative" of his landlord Alajos Sólyom, the head waiter of the Csillag hotel (earlier called *Turul* [an eagle-like symbolic figure in Hungarian popular mythology]). Sólyom had the honour of serving a cappuccino to the leader of the country and the commander-in-chief of its army. As the legend goes, Tito had a brief conversation with the ethnic Hungarian waiter:

> *afelől érdeklődött, hogy hogyan érzik magukat a magyarok a szocialista Jugoszláviában. Sokkal jobban, mint a magyarok Magyarországon, akik Sztálin csizmája alatt nyögtek, amikor meg végre fellázadtak, halomra gyilkolták őket. Vigyázzatok a testvériség-egységre, mint a szemetek fényére, válaszolta Tito marsall, mire Sólyom Lajos tiszteletudó főhajtással illette az elnököt.*
>
> 'he expressed his interest in how the Hungarians feel about their life in Socialist Yugoslavia. Much better than the Hungarians in Hungary, who were suffering under Stalin's boot and when they finally rebelled, they were killed off in masses. Keep our brotherly unity, protect it like the apple of your eye, answered Marshal Tito, to which Lajos Sólyom answered by reverently bowing his head to the president.'
> (Végel 2013, 137)

In reality, of course, nothing like that ever happened, Comrade Tito didn't pay any attention to the waiter serving him, while the hotel restaurant was populated by the officers of the secret police, "gobbling for free".

Another emblematic part of Tito's cult was the Youth Baton Relay: the baton was carried around the country every year and on the alleged birthday of Comrade Tito, May 25, solemnly given to him at a celebration at the party centre in Belgrad. The narrator, as a member of the "carefree Socialist generation", has the great honour of being allowed to run 200 meters carrying the baton, together with the same Miklós Török whose father was seen on the same notorious balcony first celebrating the arrival of the Hungarian army and later the arrival of the partisans, and by the latter first sentenced to death and then posthumously honoured. Of course, the narrator who already looks at this from the perspective of many decades and from "above", can ask such questions as "Why did we run with that baton? For whom? For what? Where?" (Végel 2013, 246), and more than half a century later, the same narrator can already say: "[...] my whole generation was like that. Innocent, naïve, and optimistic. Stupid!" (Végel 2013, 48).

List of references and sources

Ankersmit, Franklin R. 1989. *The Reality Effect in the Writing of History: The Dynamics of Historiographical Topology*. Amsterdam.

Accessed March 31, 2016. http://publishing.cdlib.org/ucpressebooks/view?docId=kt9k4016d3&chunk.id=d0e5173&toc.depth=100&toc.id=d0e5173&brand=ucpress.

Assmann, Jan. 1988. 'Kollektives Gedächtnis und kulturelle Identität.' In *Kultur und Gedächtnis,* edited by Jan Assmann and Tonio Hölscher, 9–19. Frankfurt. Accessed April 8, 2015. http://archiv.ub.uni-heidelberg.de/proplaeumdok/1895/Assmann_Kollektives_Gedeaechtnis_1988.pdf.3.

— 1992. Das kulturelle Gedächtnis: Schrift, Erinnerung und politische Identität in frühen Hochkulturen. München.

Assmann, Jan, and John Czaplicka. 1995. 'Collective Memory and Cultural Identity.' *New German Critique* 65: 125–133. Accessed March 25, 2016. http://kultura-pamieci.pl/wp-content/pliki/literatura08/assman_collective_memory.pdf.

Bence, Erika. 2008. 'Képi hidak, nyelvi hidak: metaforák, anekdoták, hazugságok.' In *A XX. század*

metaforái. Értelmezések, elemzések, bírálatok a magyar irodalom köréből, 67–77. Zenta.
— 2015. 'Ünnep(ek) Újvidéken. Végel László Neoplanta, avagy az Ígéret Földje című regényéről.' In *konTEXTUS,* Vol. 9, edited by Csányi Erzsébet, 75–89. Újvidék.
— 2015a. 'Tanú Újvidéken.' *Vár Ucca Műhely* 48: 77–82. Veszprém.
Bence, Erika. 2015b. 'Irodalmi és közéleti referenciák Mikszáth Kálmán prózaírásába.' In *Virtuális irodalomtörténet*, 33–45. Veszprém.
Dobos, István. 1995. *Alaktan és értelmezéstörténet. Novellatípusok a századforduló magyar irodalmában.* Debrecen.
Eisemann, György. 1998. *Mikszáth Kálmán.* Budapest.
Gallop, Jane. 2002. *Anecdotal Theory*. Durham. Accessed March 24, 2016. http://www.goodreads.com/book/show/567870.Anecdotal_Theory.
Gion, Nándor. 2007. *Latroknak is játszott. Virágos Katona. Rózsaméz. Ez a nap a miénk. Aranyat talált. 4 regény – Életmű I.* Budapest.
Roginer, Oszkár. 2015. *A város mint ellenérv. Újvidék a (jugoszláviai) magyar irodalomban.* Létünk könyvek 4, Szabadka.
Toldi, Éva. 2010. 'Újvidék-narratívák.' *Hungarológiai Közlemények* 3: 90–99.
Végel, László. 2013. *Neoplanta, avagy az Ígéret Földje.* Budapest.
White, Hayden. 1973. *Metahistory: the historical imagination in ninetenth-century Europe.* Baltimore. Accessed March 24, 2016. http://quod.lib.umich.edu/cgi/t/text/text-idx?c=acls;cc=acls;view=toc;idno=heb04928.0001.001

Multilingualism in the contemporary Finnish literature (Suomen kirjallisuus)

Johanna Domokos

This articile is a sightly edited version of the study *Code-switching in Suomen kirjallisuus / Finnish Literature*, orignaly published in my recent monography, Endangered Literature, L'Harmattan/KRE, Budapest, 2018, p. 81-98.

sanat am pierdut
не мога да
намеря
find söka perii
думаю
gehirnsiz[4]

1. Introduction

Writers with a multilingual background living in Finland may decide to use only one language (such as Finnish or Swedish) in their literary production, or they may choose to mix two or more languages (for example using Finnish and Sámi, or Finnish and English). This study focuses on the latter phenomenon, where writers alternate in their writings between two or more codes. Sociolinguists and linguists of multiple language acquisition have proposed several concepts for this kind of linguistic production, such as "integration" (Haugen 1953), "language interlanding" (Agheyisi 1977), "code mixing" (Bokamba 1988), or more recently "translanguaging" (Garcia and Wei 2014) and "polylanguaging" (Jørgensen et al. 2011). However, code-switching, coined by Myers-Scotton and Ury in 1977, is presently still the most frequently used term, and hence the term used for this study.

4. sanat [Finnish], am pierdut [Romanian], не мога да намеря [Bulgaria], find [English], söka[Swedish], perii [Finnish], думаю [Russia], Gehirnsiz [German, Turkish]; literary translates as: words I lost / cannot find them / find, search, try/ I am thinking / without the brain (Ståhlberg 2015, 4)

The title of this paper contains the Finnish term *Suomen kirjallisuus,* which, in addition to *suomalainen kirjallisuus,*[5] is often used in reference to Finnish literature. The literal translation of the title term takes us straight to the core of the problem, as *Suomen kirjallisuus*/ Finnish literature can indicate not only a monolingual, Finnish-language literature, but also all literature that has been written in Finland and is "of Finland". Historically viewed, the "literature of Finland" is a concept closely connected to (and motivated by) the tradition of Finnish bilingual nationalism which has included not only the Finnish but also the Finland-Swedish culture. Through this entangled[6] (multilingual, multiethnic and beyond) perspective of *Suomen kirjallisuus* we gain insights that are not apparent from the monolingual traditional perspective. And of course, for linguists and literary scholars who deal with linguistic and cultural interferences, it is absolutely inspiring to consider the aesthetics of multilingual text production in Finland.

5. As a noun phrase *Suomen kirjallisuus* contains the noun *Suomi* ('Finland') in genitive case and *kirjallisuus* ('literature') in nominative, while *suomalainen kirjallisuus* contains the adjective *suomalainen* ('Finnish') and the noun *kirjallisuus* ('literature') both in Nominative.

6. For a full definition of the term "entangled" see Sapiro 2011 and Grönstrand et al. 2014.

Thus, the general objective of this study is to investigate bilingual or multilingual writers who use two or more languages in their works, with attention to the specific types of code-switching they employ. To do this, I will adopt two types of code-switching proposed by Myers-Scotton (1993): intra-sentential (within a sentence) and inter-sentential (between sentences). In addition, I will make use of her concepts of the matrix and embedded languages, which refer to the frame or basic language, and the languages that are interspaced in between. The exemplary sample texts chosen from the past few decades of Finnish literary production will demonstrate how, on the one hand, code-switching can be covert in a literary text, and thus references to the embedded languages appear only through their translation into the main language. On the other hand, the position of the matrix language can also vary from being easily attested to complete elimination.

2. Languages-Literature-Society

In Mariane Backlén's 2001 novel *Karma* the main character writes to her Nigerian family: "Finland är ett nordeuropeiskt land, som befolkas av en mängd olika stammar, bl.a. karelarna, savolaxarna, tavastlänningarna, österbottingarna, samerna, och finlandssvenskarna" (Backlén 2001, 203). In English: "Finland is a northern European country which is inhabited by many tribes, among them the Karelians, Savonians, Tavastlander, Ostrobothnier, Sámi and the Finland-Swedes" (my transl.).

As for Finland's historical ethnic diversity, we can also add the Mishar Tatars, the Jewish and the Roma population, and the so-called "Old" Russians, i.e. Russians who settled in Finland before the 20th century. In terms of Finland's recent immigrants, who speak in excess of 150 languages, we can mention the Somalis, Estonians, Vietnamese, Iraqis, Chinese, Thais and Germans, among many others. The Ingrian Finns, the Kven and Meänkieli speakers, and Finns abroad (e.g. in Sweden, Germany, America, Australia) play a special role in the positioning of a transnational Finnish. Furthermore, is worth mentioning the Latin and Swedish writings of the forefathers of modern Finnish literature (e.g. Gabriel Porthan, Johan Ludvig Runeberg or Zachris Topelius) and the past and present works of many authors in Finland with multilingual backgrounds (Edith Södergran and other Finland-Swedish Avantgardists, Juhani Aho, Kersti Bergroth, Daniel Katz, Veijo Baltzar, Nils-Aslak Valkeapää, Sofi Oksanen, Ranya Paasonen, Kjell Westö, Sabira Ståhlberg, Bengt Pohjanen, Arja Uusitalo, Rita Magga-Kumpulainen, Cia Rinne, Sisinuke Kosola, etc.). All of these writers impose on us a wide range of linguistic and literary diversity.

Multilingualism in terms of selection and combination of languages is relevant not only for the contemporary literature of Finland. Words, sentences, whole passages of text, and even complete works in other languages appear in the history of Finnish literature. These manifestations highlight the potential of Finnish literature to expand beyond a national or monolingual identity and to welcome the linguistic and cultural diversity inherent in Finnish society. Nevertheless, the multilingual perspective within the national philological map of Finnish language and literature is practically *terra nova*. The reasons for this can be found, however, not in the marginality of the phenomenon, but in the basic construction of Finnish and comparative literary studies – both aligned as national philological approaches. Multilingualism in Finnish literature can therefore not be examined without keeping a reflective distance from the tradition of Finnish literary studies, as Heidi Grönstrand rightly points out:

> As in most nation states, there has always existed in Finland a firm connection between literature, language and nationality. In both the Finnish and Swedish speaking nationalist movements the idea of "one language – one mind" plays a strong role; often requiring from the writers to work directly or indirectly for the promotion of the specific language and culture.
> (Grönstrand 2014, 275; my transl.)

As this quote also suggests, the Finnish literature of today took root in the 19th century, the era of nationalism. In this era literature was perceived as a united voice of a monolingual nation. Similarly ethnocentric structural patterns appeared in the second half of the 20th century for the establishment of Sámi and Roma literature, and more recently for the highly vulnerable Tornedalian and Kven literature. Aside from minority or transnational authors of Finland, authors who are recent immigrants also claim much more recognition as actors in the literary life of Finland. This phenomenon shows the tendency to claim that literature should be understood as the voice of a society that is conscious of and able to celebrate and support its diversity. In addition, academic interest in multilingualism is constantly rising, as indicated by the large volume of research published on the topic by Satu Gröndahl, Eila Rantonen, Vuokko Hirvonen, Heidi Grönstrand and Kristina Malmio, Antero Leitzinger, Simo Muir, Viola Čapková-Parente, Julia Tidigs, Veli-Pekka Lehtola, Johanna Laakso and the present author. The specific topics of these studies include the multilingualism of Finnish, Sámi and Tatar writers, the literacy of the Jewish community in Finland, multilingual Finland-Swedish and Finno-Ugric authors, and the role of minorities in the construction of Finnishness.

3. Topography of voices and literary multilingualism[7]

Although the structural homology that exists between the multilingual space of Finnish society and the

7. More on this topic in Domokos (in print).

multilingual space of its literature raises interesting comparative questions, I will only discuss the issue here briefly. Similar to the topography of voices of intercultural German literature in the works of Carmine Ciellino (2000), which contains extremely diverse author groupings based on their places of origin, it is possible to map the multilingual landscape in Finnish literature in terms of six major groups comprising thirteen separate "tracks"[8]:

8. For a comprehensive literary anthology documenting the recent multicultural turn of Finnish literature through literary examples of about sixty Finnish authors see Domokos et al. 2016.

> Tracks No. 1–2 (the dominant literary fields) – Finnish and Finnish-Swedish authors who deal with cultural encounters in their books, such as Veronika Pimenov, Sinikka Nopola, Jari Tervo, Marianne Backlén, Marianne Peltomaa or Kjell Westö.
>
> Track No. 3 – indigenous Sámi authors such as Nils-Aslak Valkeapää, Kirste Paltto, Inger-Mari Aikio-Arianaick or Niillas Holmberg.
>
> Tracks No. 4–8 (historic minorities) – authors from the Roma minority, such as Veijo Baltzar or Kiba Lumberg, Jewish authors such as Daniel Katz or Mindele London, Mishar Tatars like Hassan Hamidula, Sadri Hamid or Sabira Ståhlberg, and the "old" and "new" Russians: Esa Adrian, Jana Niemi, Ljudmila Kirpu, Polina Kopylova or Zinaida Lindén.
>
> Tracks No. 9–11 – authors who migrated outside Finland (as Arja Uusitalo, Asko Sahlberg or Susanna Alakoski in Sweden), authors who are representatives of Finnish minorities, e.g. the emancipated Meänkieli authors in Sweden or Kven authors in Norway such as Bengt Pohjanen, Mikko Niemi or Alf Nilsen-Børskog and Agnes Eriksen, and repatriated Finnic authors (Raisa Lardot, Toivo Ränneli, Robert Vinonen, Ella Ojala, Arvi Perttu or Valerie Susi).
>
> Track No. 12 (with 12.a, 12.b, ...) – according to the geographical region the authors are from

– writers from diverse cultural backgrounds like Sofi Oksanen with Finnish-Estonian, Ranya Paasonen with Arabic-Finnish, or Hamdan Zakirov with Uzbek-Russian roots; the German Roman Schatz, the French-speaking Philippe Guicheteau, the Iranian Alexis Kouros, the Iraqi Hassam Blasim, the Mordvin-Russian-born Sergey Zavjalov or Roxana Crisólogo from Peru.

Track No. 13 – transitory writers who live in the country for just a short period of time but contribute to the multiculturalization of the literary landscape (e.g. Ilya Repin, Igor Severjanin, Ivan Bunin, Cia Rinne, Gerry Loose, Umayya Abu-Hanna or Inna Latiševa).

The following sections will reflect on literary code-switching in some of the works of these authors with respect to (1) grammatical structure, (2) aesthetic production, and (3) socio-cultural significance. The main argument of this study is that code-switching is a constitutive act for contemporary literature in Finland, where it repeals linguistic and cultural barriers, de-automizes semantic production, addresses the appropriation of linguistic, aesthetic and cultural diversity, and efficiently stages alterity. In the wake of the recent multicultural turn in Finnish literature, language choice is often performed programmatically, and it is systematically accompanied by poetic reflections on multilingualism. With the phenomenon of literary multilingualism, the linguistic level of the texts is increasingly put under the microscope. It becomes of great interest *how*, *when* and *why* targeted linguistic elements from phonemes to larger linguistic units and even alphabets are selected and combined in a literary work. This focus on language gives rise to reflection on the poetic function of the text, a focus valued since the formalist tradition. Moreover, research on multilingualism engages with the works of prominent scholars such as Paul de Man (1986) and Edward Said (2004), who argued that literary scholars should move beyond motif analysis to a more thorough investigation of the *language* of literature.

4. The author's choice of languages

In addition to the multilingualism of minorities and migrants, in Finland a high percentage of the population can hold a conversation in English. According to the fourth edition of EF English Proficiency Index (EF EPI), which ranks a total of 63 countries and territories, Finland is one of the top four English-speaking countries in the world (EF 2014). Many Finnish authors are fluent in more than one language and are therefore conscious of the matrix and embedded languages they choose. For example, the Finnish-Sámi authors Kirste Paltto and Nils-Aslak Valkeapää had their pamphlets published in 1970 and 1972 in Finnish, to better reach Finnish-speaking readers, but later consistently wrote only in Sámi to support the emancipatory movement of Sámi culture and the legitimization of its literary field. However, many of their works appeared in parallel Finnish or Norwegian translations. Another example is Sabira Ståhlberg, who wrote her 2006 debut novel about bullying in two parallel languages (*Molnvandraren/ Pilvivaeltaja* in Swedish and Finnish), and one of her latest children's books in four languages (*Dog weather on the Black Sea* in Finnish, Swedish, English and German, 2014). Inger-Mari Aikio-Arianaick has generally published only in Sámi, but her recent book of nature poems *Beaivváš čuohká gaba – Aurinko juo kermaa* (The sun drinks cream, 2014, published under her maiden name Inger-Mari Aikio) was written in parallel Northern Sámi and Finnish. At the opening of the Frankfurt Book Fair 2014 Sofi Oksanen also addressed the importance of language choice. Quoting a recent story, when she was asked by a journalist why she did not write in English, she underlined that she consciously wants to support the literary presence of Finnish in world literature.[9]

There are also plenty of cases in which a manuscript is published only in translation, as with the Kenyan author Joseph Owindi, whose novel *Kato, kato nekru* ('Look, Look a Negro', 1972) was originally written in English but published in his friend Risto Karlsson's Finnish translation. As in Owindi's case, many other Finnish translators, editors or publishers have aided in the publication of works by immigrant or multilingual writers. For instance, works such as Edith Södergran's poems from the early 20th century or Alexandra Salmela's 2010 novel *27 eli kuolema tekee taiteilijan* ('27, or death makes the artist')

9. See http://www.sofioksanen.com/speech-frankfurt-2014/ [02.06.2016].

were significantly edited before publication. This is not an unusual phenomenon; even the works of Finnish authors undergo serious revision by editors prior to publication, just as in developed literary fields around the globe.

While historically Edit Södergran can be considered the most polyglot figure of Finnish literature, present contenders include Sabira Ståhlberg (b. 1969) and Cia Rinne (b. 1973). In the poem *Polyglotta Politica* from *Invasion Paradies* Ståhlberg used 14 languages, and Cia Rinne used ten languages in her visual poetry collections (e.g. *Zaroum* 2001, and *Notes for Soloists* 2008).

5. Covered, reflected and overt presentation of code-switching by the narrator

When taking into consideration the level of fictional mediation, literary texts become all the more complex and elaborate compared to everyday communication. The narrator's attitude toward the languages of the narrated story is not to be underestimated, although current research has yet to investigate this issue fully. Just as in American films about Japanese geishas or samurai, Finnish literary works include scenes where the story *de facto* happens in another language, but the cinematic or literary narrator does not address this phenomenon, and the characters speak the language of the targeted audience (English in such films, or Finnish in case of Finnish books). This *zero degree code-switching*, as we might call it, allows the writer to utilize language as a medium without any special reflection, so that the audience can better focus on the storyline.

Contemporary Finnish literature is more openly addressing issues multilingualism than ever before. However, in the majority of cases the story is conveyed monolingually (which is a great help for a monolingual reader). In the following example, Sofi Oksanen provides a monolingual but self-aware description of a heteroglossic encounter. In this scene, the Estonian Aliide Truu initiates a conversation with a girl found dirty and traumatized in her garden, and the heterodiegetic narrator reports the following in Finnish:

> *Sanat sattuivat toisiinsa, kuten aiemminkin, vetäytyivät yhteen väärissä paikoissa, liittoutuivat*

ennen aikojaan, alkoivat kutittaa oudosti Aliiden korvissa. Se ei johtunut tytön sanoista eikä venäläisestä aksentista, vaan joistain muusta, tytön virossa oli muutakin outoa.
(Oksanen 2009, 18)

'The words ran together like they had before, connecting to one another in the wrong places, linking up prematurely, and they started to tickle strangely in Aliide's ear. It wasn't the girl's speech or her Russian accent, it was something else – there was something strange about her Estonian.'
(transl. by Lola Rogers 2010, 12)

In contrast to the covert multilingualism of scenes as such as this one, some authors integrate multilinguality into their works in a more overt way. Often in these cases an auto-diegetic narrator (a first-person narrator who is also the main character) relates a multilingual situation in the original languages. Here is an example from Joseph Owindi's *Kato, kato nekru* ('Look, look a Negro', 1972), a work Eila Rantonen describes as "a cold safari through the racism of the Finns… in Finland in the 1960s, when there was not more than a handful of foreigners in the country." (Rantonen 2014, 254; in my translation). When the main character is asked what is spoken at his home in Kenya, and he answers "Kiswahili," he is asked to say "I love you" in this language[10]:

10. The gray markings in this text and in further literary quotations are mine. They aim to make the relevant linguistic elements easier to notice. English translations are mine, if not else stated.

„Mimi nakupenda", minä vastaan.
„Mi … no voi sun? Voisitteko toistaa sen?"
„Mimi nakupenda. Minä vakuutan rakkauttani kärsivällisesti."
„Mimi … mitä mi … voisitteko kirjoittaa sen? On tosiaan hyvä tietää tällaisia kansanvälisiä sanoja. – Kun menen Keniaan, tulen heti tällä kielitaidollani ihmisten kanssa toimeen. Suomestahan tulee nyt kansainvälinen maa kun teikäläisiäkin asuu täällä.
(Owindi 1972, 43)

"'Mimi nakupenda", I reply.
"Mi… but how? Can you repeat that?"

"Mimi nakupenda. I patiently declare my love."
"Mimi... like, mi... could you write it down? It is certainly good to know such international expressions. – When I travel to Kenya, I will be able to manage well with these language skills. And also Finland is becoming international, as someone like you lives here.'"

6. Techniques of code-switching

It is difficult to find even a monolingual novel that does not utilize different varieties of a language. However, switching between elements of different languages within the same literary work—the key focus of this study—occurs less often. Nonetheless, code-switching can be a productive and engaging aesthetic method for staging alterity.

The following four examples are intended to illuminate both my thesis and the scalability of the code-switching. In addition to the abovementioned *zero degree* multilingualism (when the work uses one language), I will give examples of both intra-sentential and inter-sentential code-switching. The relationship between matrix language and embedded languages are further discussed in the last two examples.

6.1 Intra-sentential code-switching (1st degree code-switching)

The so called 1st degree, intra-sentential code-switching is characterized by the sporadic use of foreign words and tags in the sentences of the matrix language. They are often followed by an interpretative/explanatory word or phrase in the text. The appearance or the absence of explanatory phrases after culture-specific concepts is mostly due to the reader's degree of familiarity with the concept. Here we usually deal with the linguistic categories of *loan words* (as the words *raki* and *bulgur* in Finnish) or *foreign words* (as the words *dewi, dolmi* and *otlu peynir* in Finnish), as the example below will also show.

Layla, the 2011 novel by Jari Tervo, tells the story of a Kurdish girl who is betrothed to a Turkish man, Memed, when she is only four days old, but in the end winds up in Finland. The marriage contract between the parents is reported as follows:

He joivat sopimuksen kunniaksi dewiä, jugurttijuomaa, söivät naisten keittiöstä kantaman runsaan aterian: linssikeittoa, lammasruukun, paprikapyreellä maustettua bulguria ja dolmia, täytettyjä paprikoita.
He päättivät aterian yrtikkäällä otlu peynir -juustolla. Varsinaisen aterian jälkeen he napostelivat kuivattuja luumuja, kirsikoita, aprikooseja ja viikunoita. He tupakoivat, loikoilivat sohvalla ja katsoivat televisiota. Memed kaatoi lasiinsa rakia ja sen päälle raikasta vettä...
He kohottivat laṣiaan.
Noš, he toivottivat toisilleen.
Sulhasen maksettavaksi kuuluva başlik parasi jäi aina sulhasen isän hoidettavaksi.
(Tervo 2011, 9)

'To celebrate the agreement they drank dewi, a drink made from yogurt, and ate a wide variety of rich dishes the women brought out from the kitchen: lentil soup, lamb stew, bulgur spiced with chili paste and dolma, stuffed peppers.
They finished the food with otlu peynir cheese. After the actual meal they nibbled on dried plums, cherries, apricots and figs. They smoked, sprawled on the sofa and watched TV. Memed poured raki into his glass and refreshing water to it...
They raised their glasses.
Noš, they toasted each other.
Başlık parasi, the payment for the bride by the groom, had to be taken over by his father.'

Not only in the excerpt above, but also throughout Tervo's novel, we see the systematic insertion of elements from Turkish and Kurdish into the morphosyntactic frame of Finnish. These culturally specific lexemes and tags manifesting 1st degree code-switching, such as *dewi* (a yoghurt drink), *başlık parasi* (bride price, properly with velar ı in the first word), *otlu peynir* (herb cheese), or *noş* (with a diacritic mark below the s, rather than above), lead Finnish readers away from an automatic, plot-driven way of reading, instead bringing to foreground the arbitrary relationship between content and form (signifier and signified) of a word, while also creating awareness of a lesser-known reality. The characters with names such as Rojbin, Ibrahim, Yashar, or place names like Avcilar, Istanbul, Finnlandiya are other words that are outside the realm of everyday Finnish language, but at the same time reflect the cultural space of the characters and their unique story.

6.2 Inter-sentential code-switching (2nd degree code-switching)

In the example above, the switch from one language to another happens within the same sentence; thus, a sentence will be made up of two or more languages. However, as we see in the excerpt from Owindi above, literary texts may include whole sentences in another language. This phenomenon is commonly referred to as inter-sentential code-switching. As long as these foreign language elements do not dominate the text, it can be labeled as 2nd degree code-switching, in order to suitably place it on a scale ranging from zero embedded language to the elimination of the matrix language altogether (more the latter in upcoming examples).

In *Maija Hänninen*, the introductory chapter of Umayya Abu-Hanna's novel *Sinut* ('Thee', 2007), we find English sentences embedded in the Finnish matrix language:

> *"Kuuntele", mies sanoo ja laittaa parvekkeella olevan levysoittimen kahvan kohdalleen. LP:stä nousee laulu joka toistaa: "Niin mustalainen, niin mustalainen, niin mustalainen."*
> *Innostuneena ruova sanoo: "Oh thank you, thank you!"*
> *"Niin mus-ta-lai-nen", toistaa mies.*
> *"Oh thank you. I don't speak Finnish so I don't know what you are trying to say."*
> *Ruova heiluttaa kättä ja lähtee eteenpäin puoliksi hypellen, sillä ensimmäinen kontakti on jo saatu.*
> *Mies alkaa huutaa perään: "Gypsy, gypsy!"*
> *Pikkuruova palaa takaisin, hymyilee ja heiluttaa käsiään selittäen: "No, not Gypsy. Arab, A-RAB. I am an arab girl."*
> *Mies huutaa: "Gypsy."*

"Not Gypsy. Palestinian, you know?"
(Abu-Hanna 2007, 11)

"'Listen," said the man, bringing the needle of the record player in motion. In the song from the record it is often repeated: "So Gypsy, so Gypsy, so Gypsy."
The wuhman says excitedly: "Oh thank you, thank you!"
"So Gyyypsyyy," repeats the man.
"Oh thank you. I do not speak Finnish, so I do not know what you are trying to say."
The wuhman shakes the hand and goes on, half hopping, since the first contact has just been made.
The man begins to shout loudly: "Gypsy, gypsy"
The small wuhman turns around, smiles and waves explanatory hand: "No, not Gypsy. Arab, A-RAB. I am an Arab girl."
The man cries, "Gypsy."
"Not Gypsy. Palestinian, you know?'"

In this passage the usage of English phrases illustrates an expressive intercultural confrontation between two figures. In addition to the examples of 2nd degree, *inter-sentential code-switching* (where code-switching takes place by alternation of sentence), we see on the level of phonetics yet another example of multilingualism, namely the use of "ruova" instead of "rouva." Because the Arabic language has no diphthongs, the learner of the Finnish language has some trouble hearing and reproducing diphthongs correctly. By referring to the main character throughout the book as "ruova," the narrator emphasizes not only the seriousness but also the humorous side of the story. The same technique is also explored in Alexandra Salmela's excellent short story *Se oikea, aitoa maahanmuuttajablues* ('The Only Real Migration Blues', 2009).

In Abu-Hanna's novel, the built-in foreign phrases are in plain English. Because the majority of Finnish readers are proficient in this language, the aesthetic and socio-cultural norm of monolingualism is not so strongly disrupted. However, with the work of Sabira Ståhlberg, which will be discussed in the following section, it is important to clarify the matrix and embedded languages (cf. Myers-Scotton 1993). In diagnosing 2nd degree of code-switching, the matrix language can be easily identified as the main language of the text, into which the utterances of other languages are interwoven. However in case of *3rd degree code-switching*, sentences or phrases from other languages appear at such a high rate that the reader has difficulties telling apart the matrix language(s) and embedded language(s).

6.3 Blurring the boundary between matrix and embedded languages (3rd degree code-switching)

Sabira Ståhlberg's poem *Polyglotta Politica* contains code-switching in a radically intensive form, where the matrix language is almost deconstructed. In addition to inter-sentential code-switching, we also find examples of intra-sentential code-switching in lines five and nine, where the language changes within a single sentence. Specific cultural terms, foreign words, and sentences are not explained, as in the prose of Tervo, nor are they easy to understand, as in Abu-Hanna's novel. The code-switching in which the poetic event is located (a cruise trip in the Mediterranean) stimulates the reader to perform a language-conscious reading that allows for the pleasure of decoding and translating.

Polyglotta Politica	**Language indication**	**In English translation**
Soupe, Madame?	French	Soup, Madam?
Fish for you, Sir?	English	Fish for you, Sir?
Mehr Wein!	German	More wine!
Nous sommes une compagnie très sociable	French	We are a very sociable company.
Hey you, où est mon consommé?	English, French	Hey you, where is my consommé?
Bitte nur keine Politik	German	Please, just no politics.
The Muslims, of course the Mohammedans	English	The Muslims, of course the Mohammedans

Ahti herää, Neptunus nousee	Finnish	Ahti wakes up, Neptune rises
Ein Kreuzzug zieht durch Εὐρώπη	German, Greek	A crusade crosses Europe.
Serviette als Fahne	German	Napkin as flag
Sjöhästar ur havets djup, tilapia på tallriken	Swedish	Seahorses from the depth of the sea, tilapia on a plate
Она ужасна	Russian	It is terrible
Avledningsmanöver:	Swedish	Red herring
Madame, do you like Thai food?	English	Madame, do you like Thai food?
Pöytäliinan kastiketahra kasvaa	Finnish	The stain on the tablecloth is growing
Kastike aaltoilee *между картофите*	Finnish, Bulgarian	Wave-like sauce between potatoes
Es gibt kein Zurück.	German	There is no turning back.

Table 1. Sabira Ståhlberg. *Polyglotta Politica*

In this poem the conversation occurs between Finnish, French, English, German, Russian, Japanese, Bulgarian and Chinese-speaking passengers on a ship in the Mediterranean. The main motif, addressed from different personal perspectives, is: "They want to make us Muslims." Due to a slight preponderance of English sentences over the German, and over other less frequently used languages, as well as the repetition of the poem's main motif in English, we can consider English to be the matrix language, and the others as the embedded languages. Frequency also appears in Myers-Scotton's thesis (1993) as one of the two main criteria for identifying the matrix language of a communicative situation; however, in literature it might be more complex—a topic worth considering more in detail in future. According to Myers-Scotton, the other criterion in determining the matrix and embedded languages is the morpho-syntactic frame of the sentences. And in the examples of Abu-Hanna, Tervo and Owindi, it is indeed this principle that determines the grammatical structure of the whole text.

6.4 Homophonic translingualism (4th degree of code-switching)

The multilingual corpus of *Suomen kirjallisuus* provides us with yet another type of code-switching that is neither intra- or inter-sentential, nor it is easy to identify the matrix and embedded languages. *4th degree code-switching* is apparent in Sabira Ståhlberg's complete 2015 volume of *Polyglotta Sabirica*, as well as in many of Cia Rinne's visual poems, which often contain only one word per line, in the total absence of any larger syntactic unit. Indeed, Rinne's work creates an extreme translingual experience: on the one hand, meaning is generated by the application of multiple linguistic elements; on the other hand, the works prompt reflection on the role of letters, words, and sentences as the raw material from which literature is created, and further reflection on the role of languages as repositories of the linguistic elements that can be employed in any given work. In the example of Rinne's second book *Notes to soloists* we can see how homophony operates between languages and produces a strong drive for code-switching (2008, 5).

1
one
ohne
oh no
ono
on
o.

(oh no)
...
1 no
no.no
no)
no9
no.9
no.nine
no.nein
no.no.

N° 29
No 2 9
no two nine no to nein

from NO to NO
à luigi (nono)

NOTONO
OTONON
TONONO
ONONOT
NONOTO
ONOTON
...

As a talented descendant of Finnish-Swedish avant-gardism, as well as of Swedish and continental experimental literature, Rinne uses the selective axis of her multilingualism in order to activate the poetic function throughout her work. As formalist theoretical approaches have already proven, the paradigmatic/selective axis of language plays an important role in the poetics of a work. Rinne switches rapidly between eight and ten languages along special phonological selection methods, which strongly determine the manifestation of the poetic function in her texts. This structural similarity of both aspects—namely the use of the axes of selection in code-switching and in manifesting poetic function—underlines the essential role that code-switching can fulfill in literature.

The way Rinne's work was evaluated by the poet and literary critic Leevi Lehto says much about the significance of multilingual writing for Finnish literature:

> While you won't see her work reviewed in Finnish newspapers, or even literary magazines (the only exception being this thoughtful piece by Fredrik Hertzberg, originally published in the Swedish language Hufvudstadsbladet), to me, Cia's multilingual background alone is enough to make her an ideal utopian Finnish poet of the day – ideal in that, it really is only from a mixture of viewpoints like hers that anything like a "realistic" picture of the present "Finland" can be thought of, and

> utopian (I was about to write: tupo-ian; the Finns will get the joke) because the general respond of Finnish poetry to this "challenge of globalization" may well come to be precisely the opposite: more isolation, more Finnish-isms, and new Finnnichisms, and Finni-schisms.
> (Lehto 2005)

In this spirit as well, liberating literature from the monolingual yoke of the last two centuries can have an enlightening or even euphoric effect on readers, writers and critics, and it can lead to a more challenging complexity of the literary field. The increasing success of Cia Rinne, in spite of the early skepticism of Leevi Lehto, might prove a positive literary development in countries where Cia Rinne is active (at present, mainly Germany and Finland).

7. Conclusions

Code-switching is caused by the co-existence of languages, and it pushes the linguistic identity of literary actors to foreground simultaneously. It also increases the polyphony of the text while operating on multiple semantic levels.

Contemporary Finnish literature is distinguished not only by its preponderance of code-switching material, but also by the fact that code-switching is used deliberately and programmatically, and it is systematically accompanied by poetic reflections. The recent increasing number of multilingualism/code-switching in Finnish literature urges linguistics, literature, and cultural studies to meet Finnish Studies in order to better understand this versatile phenomenon in all of its structural, aesthetic, and functional complexity. Additionally, this interdisciplinary approach could form a contribution to the establishment of an intercultural Finnish studies on a longer run.

Mapping the social and literary context of this phenomenon reveals that code-switching is a constitutive act for contemporary literature in Finland. It repeals linguistic and cultural barriers, de-automizes semantic production, addresses the appropriation of linguistic, aesthetic and cultural diversity, and stages alterity efficiently.

The above reflections on literary code-switching with respect to its grammatical structure, its aesthetic production, and to its socio-cultural significance resulted in the differentiation of five code-switching techniques applicable not only to Finnish literature but to other literatures as well. In placing types of code-switching on a scale of 4 degrees, the types of intra- and inter-sentential code-switching as well as the concepts of the matrix and embedded languages proposed by Myers-Scotton (1993) were implemented. These numbered code-switching degrees allow us to scale the multilingual qualities of a literary text from covert to overt manifestations, as well as from the covert usage of the embedded language (0 degree) to the use of a few foreign words (1st degree) and some sentences (2nd degree), up to a high number of embedded language units (3rd degree), and finally, the complete disappearance of the matrix language (4th degree).

This study employed concepts from linguistics (code-switching) and literary theory (experimental literature and poetic language) in order to contribute to the mapping of multilingualism in contemporary literature in Finland, as well as to enhance the methodology of literary code-switching. Crucially, however, the degrees of code-switching outlined in this study are not only applicable to Finnish literature. By employing this analytical framework in other literary fields, we can gain further proof of how strongly literary code-switching underlines the materiality of language, alphabets, and grammar, thus gaining new insights into the connections between the verbal, the poetic, and the world around us.

List of references and sources

Abu-Hanna, Umayya. 2007. *Sinut.* Helsinki.

Agheyisi, Rebecca. 1977. 'Language Interlarding in the Speech of Nigerians.' In *Language and Linguistic Problems in Africa*, edited by Paul F. A. Kotey and Hain Der-Houssikian, 99–110. New York.

Backlén, Marianna. 2001. *Karma.* Helsinki.

Bokamba, Eyamba. 1988. 'Code Mixing, Language Variation and Linguistic Theory: Evidence from Bantu languages.' *Lingua* 76: 21–62.

Ciellino, Carmine. 2000. 'Einleitung: Eine Literatur des Konsenses und der Autonomie – Für eine

Topographie der Stimmen.' In *Interkulturelle Literatur in Deutschland. Ein Handbuch*, edited by Carmine Ciellino, 51–263. Stuttgart, Weimar.

de Man, Paul. 1986. 'The return to philology.' In *The resistance to theory*, 3–26. Minneapolis.

Domokos, Johanna. Ed. 2013a. *Finnek_? Tanulmányok a multikulturális Finnországról.* [Reader on multicultural Finland]. Győr.

— Ed. 2013b. *Finnek_! Multikulturális finn irodalmi olvasókönyv.* [Reader on multicultural Finnish literature]. Győr.

— Ed. 2014. *Invasion Paradies. Lesebuch über die Möglichkeiten, Finne zu sein. Ein multikulturelles Plädoyer*. Budapest.

— 2018. *A writing hand reaches further. Evaluation of Sámi literature. Culture for all. Kultuuria Kaikille.* https://multilingualmonth.files.wordpress.com/2018/10/writing_hand_reaches_further_verkko.pdf

— 2018. *Endangered literature.* L'Harmattan/KRE. Budapest (2018)

— 2018 *Multicultural Dynamics and the Finnish Literary Field.* In Gröndahl, S. and Rantonen, E. (eds) Migrants and Literature in Finland and Sweden. Helsinki: Finnish Literature Society. DOI: https://doi.org/10.21435/sflit.11

Domokos, Johanna, Sanna Grund, Heidi Grönstrand, Hanna-Leena Nissilä, and Sabira Ståhlberg. Eds. 2016. *Maailma kotona. Kohtaamsen opas.* Varna.

EF. 2014. *'English Proficiency Index.'* Accessed July 7, 2016. http://www.ef.com/epi.

Garcia, Ofelia and Li Wei. 2014. *Translanguaging. Language, Bilingualism and Education.* New York.

Grönstrand, Heidi. 2014. 'Sprachgrenzen verschieben sich, Literaturauffassungen verändern sich – oder doch nicht?' In *Invasion Paradies,* edited by Johanna Domokos, 274–289. Budapest.

Grönstrand, Heidi, Mikko Pollari, Hanna-Leena Nissilä, Kukku Melkas, Oli Löytty, and Ralf Kauranen. (in print). 'National, transnational and entangled literatures: Methodological considerations focusing on the case of Finland.' In *Rethinking*

National Literatures and the Literary Canon in Scandinavia, edited by Ann-Sofie Lönngren, Heidi Grönstrand, Dag Heede, and Anne Heith, 2–29. Cambridge.

Gröndahl, Satu. Ed. 2002. 'Litteraturens gränsland. Invandrar- och minoritetslitteratur i nordiskt perspektiv.' *Uppsala Multiethnic Papers* 45.

Haugen, Einar. 1953. 'The analysis of linguistic borrowings.' *Language* 26: 210–231.

Hirvonen, Vuokko. 2008. *Voices from Sápmi. Sámi Women's Path to Authorship*. Translated by K. Anttonen. Guovdageaidnu.

Jørgensen, J. Normann, Martha Sif Karrebæk, Lian Malai Madsen, and Lian Malai Møller. 2011. 'Polylanguaging in Superdiversity.' *Diversities Journal* 18 (3): 32–54.

Kilchmann, Esther. 2012. 'Poetik des fremden Worts. Techniken und Topoi heterolingualer Gegenwartsliteratur.' *Zeitschrift für interkulturelle Germanistik* 3 (2): 109–129.

Lehto, Leevi. 2005. 'Awkward Thoughts on a Gracious Book.' Accessed June 6, 2016. http://leevilehto.net/?s=Awkward+Thoughts+on+a+Gracious+Book.

Myers-Scotton, Carol. 1993. *Social Motivation for Code-Switching: Evidence from Africa*. Oxford.

Myers Scotton, Carol, and William Ury. 1977. 'Bilingual Strategies: The Social Functions of Code-Switching.' *International Journal of the Sociology of Language* 13: 5–20.

Oksanen, Sofi. 2009. *Puhdistus*. Helsinki.

— 2010. *Purge*. Translated by Lola Rogers. New York.

— 2014. Santa Clause speaks Finnish. Accessed June 6, 2016.

— http://www.sofioksanen.com/speech-frankfurt-2014/.

Owindi, Joseph. 1972. *Kato, kato nekru*. Helsinki.

Rantonen, Eila. Ed. 2010. *Vähemmistöt ja monikulttuurisuus kirjallisuudessa*. Tampere.

— 2014. 'Literatur von Immigranten in Finnland.' In *Invasion Paradies*, edited by Johanna Domokos, 254–273. Budapest.

Rinne, Cia. 2001. *Zaroum*. Helsinki.

— 2008. *Notes for soloists*. Koppenhagen.
Said, Edward W. 2004. *Humanism and Democratic Criticism*. New York.
Sapiro, Gisèle. 2011 'Comparativism, Transfers, Entangled History: Sociological Perspectives on Literature.' In *A Companion to Comparative Literature*, edited by Ali Behdad and Dominic Thomas, 231–232. Chichester.
Ståhlberg, Sabira. 2006. *Pilvinvaelatja*. Helsinki.
— 2006. *Molnvandrarer*. Helsinki.
— 2014. 'Polyglotta Politica.' In Invasion Paradies, edited by Johanna Domokos, 206–211. Budapest.
— 2014. *Dog Weather on the Black Sea*. Varna
— 2014. *Hundewetter auf dem Schwarzmeer*. Varna.
— 2014. *Кучешко време в Черно море*. Varna.
— 2014. *Koiran elämä Mustamerellä*. Varna.
— 2015. *Polyglotta Sabirica*. Varna.
Salmela, Alexandra. 2009. 'Se oikea, aitoa maahanmuuttajablues.' In *Mikä ihmeen uussuomalainen?*, edited by Maarit Halmesarka, Olli Löytty, and Mikko Rimminen, 35–55. Helsinki.
— 2010. *27 eli kuolema tekee taiteilijan*. Helsinki.
Tervo, Jari. 2011. *Layla*. Helsinki.

Hungarian Migrant Writers in the West since 1945

Károly Kókai

1. Introduction

Since the end of the Second World War there has been considerable migration from Hungary to the West. For historical reasons we used to subdivide the period "since 1945" further, with the system change of 1989 as the turning point. Taking a closer look the period 1945–1989 proves to be a period marked by overwhelming diversity.[11]

11. For comments on the previous versions of this paper I am indebted to Johanna Laakso, Johanna Domokos and Satu Gröndahl.

The migration between 1945 and 1989, in the period of the state socialism in Hungary and of the Cold War internationally, must be considered as a specific case for many reasons. The cause of the migration was political, hence we have to name it "exile": the migrants were forced by political oppression in their home country to leave, they hoped for political changes – or even worked to effect these changes – and consequently, they hoped for the possibility to return. Secondly, during the 44 years under consideration the situation in Hungary – as well as in the countries the migrants moved to – changed.

The migrants adapted to their new circumstances. They reflected the new and changing situation in their work, wrote mainly or exclusively for a new audience, that is, for the other migrants or for the readership of their host countries and only partially, if at all, for the audience of the country they had left behind. Thirdly, between 1945 and 1989 there was continuous emigration. For didactic reasons we talk about migration waves, such as "the 1948 migration" or "the 1956 migration", but since literary studies deals with individual texts and individual authors, every case has to be considered in its singularity. Thus, this migration, bound together by the historic situation of the Cold War, nevertheless has to be seen in its variety and diversity. Similarly (and fourthly), the migrant authors used a wide range of literary structures. They founded newspapers and magazines, organized conferences and literary performances, distributed their texts in every significant form from oral to print, and joined established organizations such as broadcasting companies. They founded their own societies and joined existing ones: György Sebestyén, for instance, became president of the writer's association "PEN Club" of Austria. Migration shaped every aspect of their literature. The infrastructure of production and distribution, the stories told, the languages used, the public addressed, as well as the aesthetics of the texts were formed by it. The specificity of this migration shows thus a linguistic as well as a cultural complexity.

All details of this complexity cannot be discussed or even listed in a short paper. I choose in the following a few examples to be able to take a closer look to a few significant elements of this complexity. The life stories of the authors, their cultural backgrounds, and their ways in the societies and literary worlds of their host countries show not only picturesque and anecdotal details, but also enable us to analyze the very structures of the migration as well as the (literary and language) cultures in which they are to be placed. This paper is divided into two parts. The first introduces individual examples and thus considers writers "on their own". The second part addresses theoretical problems using the examples introduced in the first. Since the theoretical framework addressed in the second part has been widely discussed in recent years, it is advisable to start with the individual examples.

2. Three examples for the literature of migration

In the following, I will discuss the literature of migration using three examples. Sándor Márai, György Sebestyén and Agota Kristof differ in many respects: not only in age and gender but also in what stage of their literary career they left Hungary, in which community they tried to find their places, and thus, for whom they wrote.

Any attempt to describe the host culture as well as the migrant culture where Márai, Sebestyén and Kristof acted, based on the evidence of their personal stories and their literary work, would provide us with three entirely different pictures. The aim of this paper is to ask whether it is possible to discuss these pictures in the categories of multiculturalism and multilingualism. Márai, Sebestyén and Kristof not only used different languages – in their everyday life as well as in their work as writers – but they reflected these multilingualisms in their texts as well. They decided on one language and developed a special version of it. Márai used an increasingly outdated Hungarian, Sebestyén created a slightly artificial German existing only in his books, and Kristof turned to the reduced French of a 12-year-old. The choice of these languages are on the one hand explainable by the biographies of these authors and they contribute to the literary value of their work on the other. The consciousness for a private language was clearly shaped by the situation of working in a multilingual situation. Since migrants form their own world with only weak and most importantly fresh roots in their new social world – making a significant difference to the traditional minorities, struggling over generations within a culture dominated by majorities – the sensitivity for this kind of multilingualism forms one of the artistic problems migrant authors have to deal with.

Multiculturalism takes similarly specific forms in the case of migrants. Migrants represent with their sheer existence a different cultural form than that of the host society, if in no other respect, with the distinctive features of the ways in which they arrived. Migration involved in the period of the Cold War existential decisions, many times dangers or at least the fear of dangers, and included persecution or the flight from persecution. In any case it forced all involved to take sides and to bear the consequences of the decisions made. Altogether, it created a situation to deal with existentially, psychologically and artistically for a whole life. Taking this common background into consideration helps us to summarize the cases of Márai, Sebestyén and Kristof.

Sándor Márai left Hungary 1948 after a successful career spanning many decades that had started in the early 1920s. He was forced to realize that there was no place for him in the Stalinist cultural field of the new regime – or rather, only one: the role of the class enemy. Márai moved to Italy and worked for Radio Free Europe in Munich, a Cold War propaganda instrument of US state organizations. He moved then to the US, spending the last years of his life in San Diego, California. His personal life and literary career is a classic example of an emigrant writer. Márai did not switch language, despite the fact that he had grown up bilingual (German and Hungarian) and had had literary success in the West before the Second World War. It can be seen as a symbolic act that he killed himself in the beginning of the year of the system change which ended the state socialist period in Hungary. The reasons were personal, as we know from his diary[12] but his death nevertheless marks the impossibility of returning from exile. He became one of the best-known Hungarian authors in the West during the 1990s and 2000s. His most successful text is *Embers*, written in 1942 and dealing with a past far away from the realities of its recent readers. After his death in 1989 the success of Márai is not surprising due to his qualities as a writer but because of the worldview he transports into his texts. It is a nostalgic picture of a glorified past with stories centered on the values of an imagined well-to-do middle class.

12. His two closest relatives, Lola (Ilona Matzner), his wife, and János, his adopted son, mentioned in his text further below as "L." and as "child", had died; Márai was 89 and alone.

György Sebestyén – my second example, mentioned before as the president of the Austrian writers' organization – arrived in Austria at the end of 1956. Shortly afterwards he visited the bureau of the Austrian writers' organizations, where he met the secretary Erika Hanel. Sebestyén became a contributor of the Hungarian language newspaper *Magyar Híradó* ('Hungarian News') produced by Hungarian refugee journalists, financed by channels of the institutions of Austrian civil societies, and distributed among the Hungarian refugees in Austria, and worked on the Novel *Die Türen schliessen sich* ('Closing doors'). He started to work on this text in Budapest during the days of the uprising of October/November 1956 and finished it a few months later in Austria. The text was translated into German with the help of Erika Hanel and published 1957.[13] Sebestyén continued to work for *Magyar Híradó*, even becoming its editor, but his aim was to become an "Austrian writer". He soon switched languages and created a specific identity.

Agota Kristof considered herself a Hungarian writer in exile. She found herself after her emigration 1956 in a socially and linguistically hostile environment. She published Hungarian poems in the Paris-based magazines *Magyar Műhely* ('Hungarian Studio') and *Irodalmi* Újság[14] ('Literary News') and become silent for many years, working in a watch factory in Switzerland and learning the local language. She achieved literary success after writing a book in the French adapted from her 12-year-old son. Thus, Kristof took advantage of her problem of trying to write in a foreign language. According to the plot of *The Notebook* (published in French 1986 as *La grand cahier*) the two brothers, whose notebook we read, agree to the use of a reduced language to avoid all personal involvement and concentrating only on facts. The idea for this simplified French came, as Kristof told in interviews, after reading a short essay of her 12-year-old son wrote for a school class. However what is obvious in case of Kristof goes for all three writers discussed here: they struggled for a language adequate to express their situation as migrant writers in a multilingual and multicultural environment, an environment in which their native language and culture clashed with the majority language and culture of their respective host countries.

The contraposition of Márai on the one hand, writing during his exile in Hungarian, and Sebestyén and Kristof on the other, switching to other languages, should not disguise the fact that none of these writers writes in the language he/she speaks. Writing differs from spoken language significantly. That is obvious, for example, in the cases of Baroque epic poems. Prose and the effort to

13. The extent of Erica Hanel's influence on the text *Die Türen schliessen sich* is hard to determine, since there are no records of her discussions with Sebestyén and since she did not produce any notable literary works of her own.

14. *Irodalmi Újság* was published 1957-1961 in London, 1962-1989 in Paris.

write in a "natural way" can disguise, but cannot change, this fact. Literature is the artificial use of elements of so-called mother tongues.

Looking at these three authors, it becomes obvious that they lived for decades in a common world, that of the Hungarian migrant writers. They published works for a similar public, that is, the Hungarian migrants as well as (in the case of Sebestyén and Kristof directly, in the case of Márai indirectly, that is, through translations) for the local public of the host country – and they knew virtually nothing of each other. All three tried to go their own way and had success doing so, finding effective literary expression of the common problem, of being an Eastern European migrant writer in the West.

Another common feature is that their lives as well as their literary work were shaped by the very act of migration itself. This act divided not only their worlds in two halves, and made cultural transfer to central issues of their intellectual activities, but formed focal points of their writings as well. The cultural transfer relevant for Márai, Sebestyén and Kristof means here not only the translations of texts, the contributions in the distribution of cultural ideas and achievements of one culture in to other, but more importantly of all the artistic intensity arising from the intimate knowledge of different cultures and of the difficulties of their compatibility. All three, Márai, Sebestyén, and Kristof, told stories of the very act of migration. They described the crossing of a border or at least the moment of remaining on the threshold. The following three passages are concentrating on this very act. They make visible not only the centrality of the act itself but also the struggles to find the adequate literary form for its depiction. The three quotations are taking from significantly different points in the texts. Márai is starting in his diary a new autobiographic story with the event of crossing the border, and Sebestyén and Kristof are ending their fictions with it. Nevertheless, in each three cases it is obvious that we are confronted with an act marking a point of no return.

Márai:
"September 7, 1948. With L. and the child in Geneva for four days. Two strong memories from

the journey. The one: the Hungarian detective at the border, looking at our passports, and saying gently: Good-bye. With a tone of resignation, unforgettable. The other: the young Russian soldier, after midnight, in the train waiting on the bridge over the Enns – this marked the end of the Iron Curtain – stepped into the sleeping car, took and returned our passports, and gave us a salute without a word. I can remember his face. The other started in this moment, which – I am sure now – will last a very long time."[15]
(The full diary 1948, 252)

15. All translations are by Károly Kókai.

Sebestyén:
"Zoltán stood in the open door and looked out into the square. The rattling crash of the receding tank faded, becoming entirely silent. Burnt rags wafted in the air softly gleaming in the light as if black copper leafs. From the car, no flames came out anymore. Thin and blue smoke rose between the wedged metal plates. Of the four mounds on the pavement, three were black; the smoldering cloth seemed to move in the hot air. The fourth figure was pale like ivory, no smoke came from it, nothing moved on it."
(Closing doors 1957, 319)

Kristof:
"Father takes two wooden boards, goes forward, leans one of the boards against the fence, climbs. We lie down behind the big three, we keep our ears close by both hands, we open our mouths. There is an explosion. We run with the other wooden boards and with the cloth bundle to the fence. Father lies on the second fence. Taking the cloth bundle, stepping in the footsteps, climbing over the dead body, one of us goes in to the other land."
(The notebook 1986, 187)

All three authors developed a literary body-of-work based on this experience of staying on the threshold while crossing the border. Márai published his diaries reflecting an outside world passing by. Sebestyén created an oeuvre based on his Central Europeanness, including both sides of the Iron Curtain. Kristof published a trilogy telling the story of the siblings separated at the fence.

Márai, Sebestyén and Kristof represent the diversity of Hungarian migration to the West, a diversity defining a field. They were connected not only by exile and a common trauma but also by the struggles that led to their exile, as well as by the struggles with the cultural environment in which they worked. In these three examples, multilingualism and multiculturalism take on a specific meaning. It is the condition of working on an identity, creating a literary text, developing an oeuvre.

3. Theoretical Problems

At the same time, in the context of a panel at a Finno-Ugric conference on Multilingualism and Multiculturalism in Finno-Ugric Literatures the question arose: can we discuss the culture of migration in the same categories as the culture of minorities? Do multilingualism and multiculturalism mean the same thing with regard to the migrants and with regard to the autochthonous minorities? This question becomes even sharper if we consider the cultural, economic and political situation of the Finno-Ugric majorities and minorities in Finland, Hungary and Estonia as well as in Russia on the one hand, contrasted with the case of migrants discussed here on the other. Wouldn't a comparison to the other Central European migrants to the West during the period of the Cold War be better? The point for which this paper argues for is that the culture of migration is a complex one and it would be an inexcusable distortion to reduce it to one of its political dimensions, that of the protest against the Stalinist, Communist, and socialist regimes of Hungary after the Second World War. An approach from the exact opposite direction proves to be adequate. We have to consider culture itself as an inhomogeneous complexity, understandable only by analysing its structures from the viewpoints of its others, for example of its minorities.

One of the issues seems to be finding the scientific methods, the appropriate concepts, the suitable theories to deal with these problems. Can, for example, post-colonial theories be used to discuss the literature of Márai, Sebestyén and Kristof? Are the concepts of

Edward Said (orientalism)[16], Homi Bhabha (third space, hybridity)[17] or Gayatri Spivak (subalternity)[18] of any use with respect to the Hungarian migrant writers in the West? If we take the post-colonial theories as a means of becoming open to the perspectives of migrants and to understand the cultural mechanisms at work in "the West", these concepts prove useful. They help us to understand the situation of the migrant writers, to give meaning to the language shifts, as well as to the refusal of it, and to understand the dynamics of multilingualism and multiculturalism. They help us to differentiate between the cases of Kristof, Sebestyén and Márai. The grades of applicability of the concept of the third space in which the writer is working are for example, in the case of Kristof, much higher in comparison to Sebestyén or Márai. Kristof developed her own language – and that is the language of subaltern subjects – appropriate for her third space. The third space of Márai was that of a writer in exile, which explains why he was not only exiled from communist Hungary but from the rapidly modernizing West as well. Sebestyén adapted to the new language with the help of Erika Hanel, who translated his text under the pseudonym of Lena Dur, creating the third space of a language invented by a couple.

In the case of Hungarian migrant writers' orientalism, a concept heavily used in post colonial studies, is maybe not an issue, but exoticism is. This was instrumentalised by the authors themselves, for example by Sebestyén in the stories he told, in the figures he created, as well as in his pseudo identity as "centaur from the lands of the Danube."

Hibridity describes the work of all three authors in focus here. As migrants, they mixed elements of their native and host cultures creating a new one, unique and understandable only in itself. Since the culture of Hungary on the one hand, and the cultures of Italy and the US, Austria, as well as Switzerland and France on the other, the countries where Márai, Sebestyén and Kristof worked, differs not in the scale as the culture of the former colonising countries from the one of the colonised – in the case of Bhabha, who invented the concept of hybridity in the cultural sciences, that of England and India – hybridity takes here a specific meaning. A further

16. Said, Edward. 1978. *Orientalism*. New York.

17. Bhabha, Homi. 1994. *The location of culture*. London.

18. Spivak, Gayatri. 1988. 'Can the subaltern speak?' In *Marxism and the interpretation of culture*, edited by Cary Nelson and Lawrence Goldberg, 271-313. Chicago.

point is that the culture of Hungary was developed over centuries long in an engagement with western cultural influences, from the introduction of the Roman Catholic Christianity in the 10th century to the western type modernisms of recent times, so there is in the native culture of the listed authors a living tradition of adapting to western cultural standards. In the cases of Márai, Sebestyén and Kristof hybridity is therefore rather a tool of the cultural sciences to be used to isolate and analyse elements of their literary works. The concept of hybridity allows, for example, for an understanding of the conflict of Márai refusing the contemporary culture of the West – and that means in his *Diary 1944–1957* the culture of James Joyce, Franz Kafka, Wystan Hugh Auden and Thomas Stearns Eliot – as conflict keeping an identity as emigrant and not interpreting it as a simple conservatism. What Márai tried to concentrate on were Hungarian classics like Dezső Kosztolányi, János Arany and Mihály Vörösmarty, "timeless" poets of the 1830s – 1930s, an imaginary world of pure literature disconnected from reality. Hybridity took up therefore specific forms here, forms, in reverse, can only be explained by concepts like hybridity. The concepts of postcolonial theories, like third space, exoticism, subalternity, and hybridity, can thus be used to understand the culture of migrants, because these concepts approach culture as an inhomogeneous one, put together from inconsistent elements. Culture is in reality driven by the energies provided by the confrontation – or rather encounter – of components not fitting.

The central question regards thus the structures of that which we call "culture." According to a possible and extremely simplified concept of culture, this means a homogeneous field defined by one language, a clearly shaped geographical area, a community of people bond together by mutual solidarity, a historical tradition accepted by all members of the community, and as a result, by a well-defined identity. A next definition includes minorities, that is, structures it according to majorities and minorities. According to this view the majority as well as the minority defines themselves by differentiating the one from the other. A third and naturally complicated definition includes not only the legally recognized or so-called traditional, that means since generations in a specific geographic are living minorities, but migrants too. In this way the picture becomes even more complex, allowing on the one hand for the development of the irrational concepts of homogeneous national identities threatened by hostile neighbors as well as by inner enemies like old and new migrants.[19] However on the other hand, the inclusion of migrants in the definition of culture allows to reach a level of differentiations, which changes the paradigm. The aim is no longer to keep culture close, but on the contrary: to understand it as a field of inclusion. The approval of such a diversified field allows for the understanding of specific identities, like for example, those of the migrants.

19. For details see the recent discussions of right wing ideologies from the True Finns to the Jobbik, that is The Better Ones, which regardless of the lacking of any significant number of new migrants in Finland or in Hungary succeed to work with artificially awakened fears of nationalistic hostilities.

For all three authors the decisive factor seems to be thus: their cultural adaptation to the new environments happened by means of the conservation of the memories of traumatic experiences. The cultural transfer was mutual, but first formed by the need of the author to give witness, to reflect on his/her confrontation with the new environment and with a fading past, and thus to problematize the act and the reasons for his/her migration. The literary work was shaped by the constructing of an identity, that of the migrant writers.

The three cases discussed in this paper were specific in the sense that they were only possible in a unique historical situation, that of the Cold War. Nevertheless, considering the number of migrants, this period seems to be far from extraordinary. According to recent[20] estimations, about 500,000 Hungarians have left the country over the last ten years, more than in any other decade since 1945.[21] Therefore, it is not the number but the political relevance that the Cold War gave the migration between 1945 and 1989 that is specific.

20. That is: August 2015.

21. Or rather: approximately the same as in the late 1940s, when a great number of the members of the German minority in Hungary were deported to the West.

A further peculiarity of the migrants in comparison to autochthonous minorities is that the fading away happens within one generation. That is what shaped the literary oeuvres of these three authors. The next generation of migrants are not the children of the first – because they are assimilated into the host culture of their parents – but the next migrants of the coming decades.

The literary products of the migrant writers belong to the culture of the host as well as to their home country – thematically and biographically as well as bearing witness to specific forms of multilingualism and multiculturalism.

Nevertheless, these features seem to be only individual details of a much larger whole. When discussing the Hungarian migrant writers in the West between 1945 and 1989 it seems to be meaningful to use the same categories as in the case of minority cultures. Migration literature is a specific form of minority literature. Given the fact that each and every "language" is a bundle of different languages which differ chronologically (e.g. Hungarian before and after the language reforms of the early 19th century), regionally (dialects), socially (the languages of different social strata and professional groups), and stylistically (the language of literature and that of everyday use), the difference between majority and minority languages seems to be a political construction.[22] If we focus on the meaning of the other concept, that of multiculturalism, by discussing migrant and minority cultures, what becomes visible is the same again: the multidimensionality of culture itself, an inherent quality of the very concept.

22. In this - political - sense, the construction is naturally a decisive one, since it means survival or disappearance, namely for both the autochthonous minority and the migrants.

Discussing minority and migrant literature and taking a closer look at specific literary oeuvres provides us with the opportunity to understand the structures and working mechanisms of the host cultures. Everybody is confronted with his environment and has to deal with the established cultural trends and structures of production. Migrant writers are different only in that they experience these confrontations more sharply. Their success and failure therefore make the possibilities and the limits of the cultural system more visible – whereas the case of Márai makes it clear that what is considered failure from the viewpoint of the host culture can be a success from the perspective of the migrant. The possibilities discussed in this paper were the adaptation and rejection of language, of actual cultural trends, of structures of production. Márai rejected the structures of the writers' organizations of the countries in which he lived, while Sebestyén eagerly grabbed his first opportunity to get involved and rose to the top of the Austrian Writers' Organization. Both struggled with the existing structures in their own way, and that is why their careers invite analysis. The delay of the literary success of Kristof can be analyzed for the same purposes, demonstrating that it is rather the untypical career trajectories that reveal the decisive structures. Migration and being a migrant thus shaped all aspects of the literature of Márai, Sebestyén and Kristof, its languages, subjects and genres, its production, distribution and reception. Taking three examples belonging together only in terms of very basic characteristics – migrant writers of Hungarian origin in the Cold War era – demonstrates that the observations collected in this paper are not case-specific but precisely the opposite: they point to the general and dominant determinants.

List of references and sources

Bhabha, Homi. 1994. *The Location of Culture*. London.

Kristof, Agota. 1986. *Le grand cahier*. Paris.

Márai, Sándor. 2008. *Teljes napló 1948*. Budapest.

Said, Edward. 1978. *Orientalism*. New York.

Sebestyén, György. 1957. *Die Türe schliessen sich*. Wien.

Spivak, Gayatri. 1988. 'Can the subaltern speak?' In *Marxism and the interpretation of culture*, edited by Cary Nelson, and Lawrence Goldberg, 271–313. Chicago.

Multilingualism in Finno-Ugric minority literatures: authenticity vs. emancipation?

Johanna Laakso

1. Mothers or midwives of language and literature: documenting authenticity or creating a language of one's own?

In this paper, I will try to approach the questions of multilingual writing from the point of view of Finno-Ugric minority languages and the literature written in these languages. So far, the presence of minority languages in multilingual writing has often been regarded from the point of view of major or dominant languages. The question is how occasional words and phrases in a minority language are inserted into texts which are targeting dominant-language readership, including readers who do not even understand the minority language in question – for example, what is the role of the occasional Meänkieli or Finnish elements in the Swedish-language novels by today's Swedish authors such as Mikael Niemi or Susanna Alakoski. Sometimes (as in linguistic landscape studies) such texts are even investigated by researchers who don't know the minority language at issue (see e.g. Jonsson 2012) and may exaggerate the importance of its presence.

In fact, the indexical and symbolic use of occasional minority-language items "spicing" the text as in Mikael Niemi's *Popular Music* analysed by Jonsson (2012) is probably very far from real-language multilingualism as minority speakers themselves experience it. For a reader who understands Finnish or Meänkieli, Niemi's occasional Finnish or Meänkieli words are very few and far between, especially in relation to the fact that language issues are discussed and commented on very conspicuously – but mostly in Swedish – throughout the novel. These minority-language items represent the usual fields of symbolic and socially indexical uses (address words, greetings and other ritualized phrases, ethnographic and culinary terms; cf. Jonsson 2012, 221); they provide the "local colour" with its illusory distinctiveness (cf. Kapor 2009, 76), without really challenging the reader, and one could claim that, from the point of view of the majority readership, they, instead of "making silenced voices heard", might just as well serve to reproduce the "self-consolidating otherness" in Gayatri Spivak's sense, strengthening the subject position of a privileged inhabitant of neo-colonial space (Huddart 2008, 142). I will try to take another angle and sketch some approaches to multilingualism as it appears in minority-language literature, especially from the point of view of authenticity and the role of language use in ethnolinguistic emancipation.

Most of the Finno-Ugric minority languages have only been used in writing since the late 19th or early 20th century or even later, and some of them are still in the process of being standardized for literary use. At the same time, this process of standardization and literarization is their best, or perhaps even only, means of emancipation in a world and a linguistic culture in which a "real" language, a language deserving recognition, is a language of written literature.

On many scales of endangerment or emancipation, the use of the language at issue in literature as an indicator of language maintenance is positioned somewhere in-between the most critical state of endangerment (in which the language often only lives as a spoken vernacular in the private sphere) and secured maintenance (in which the language is used across all informal and formal domains). For instance, as early as the 1950s, Heinz Kloss described the profile of the Ausbau of a new language: at the first stage, the language is used for humorous or folkloristic purposes, "in a fool's gown", then in poetry, then in so-called Zweckschrifttum or serious prose, and finally in technical and scholarly texts and in public administration (Kloss 1952, 28; quoted in Haugen 1966, 930). On the EGIDS scale created by Lewis and Simons on the basis of Fishman's famous GIDS and used in the Ethnologue database, between the two extremes – level 0, wide national and international use, and level 10, completely extinct – the use of the language at issue in literature characterizes the intermediate levels 5 (Developing) and 4 (Educational).

Level	**Label**	**Description**
0	International	The language is widely used between nations in trade, knowledge exchange, and international policy.
1	National	The language is used in education, work, mass media, and government at the national level.
2	Provincial	The language is used in education, work, mass media, and government within major administrative subdivisions of a nation.
3	Wider Communication	The language is used in work and mass media without official status to transcend language differences across a region.
4	Educational	The language is in vigorous use, with standardization and *literature* being sustained through a widespread system of institutionally supported education.

5	Developing	The language is in vigorous use, with *literature* in a standardized form being used by some though this is not yet widespread or sustainable.
6a	Vigorous	The language is used for face-to-face communication by all generations and the situation is sustainable.
6b	Threatened	The language is used for face-to-face communication within all generations, but it is losing users.
7	Shifting	The child-bearing generation can use the language among themselves, but it is not being transmitted to children.
8a	Moribund	The only remaining active users of the language are members of the grandparent's generation and older.
8b	Nearly Extinct	The only remaining users of the language are members of the grandparent's generation or older who have little opportunity to use the language.
9	Dormant	The language serves as a reminder of heritage identity for an ethnic community, but no one has more than symbolic proficiency.
10	Extinct	The language is no longer used and no one retains a sense of ethnic identity associated with the language.

Table 1. Expanded Graded Intergenerational Disruption Scale[23]

23. From Lewis et al. 2016; emphasis by J.L.

However, for many Finno-Ugric minority languages, literary use represents the highest level of maintenance they can expect to achieve. With few exceptions, such as some parts of the Saami area, most Finno-Ugric minority peoples are a minority even in their titular administrative areas, and in most public domains (mass media, public administration, most workplaces, etc.) the state language dominates, despite the mostly modest attempts at revitalization policies (for Russia, see especially Zamyatin 2014). This means that literature alongside other specific ethnocultural frameworks (for instance, certain restricted parts of mass media and education) is one of the very few public domains in which these languages can be used in writing.

An author writing in an endangered language of this kind is playing a dual role: both reproducing an authentic, existing language and creating it, bringing it into existence – because in our modern world, only in written literature can a language really exist. Languages without literary forms and literacy practices will be reduced to the role of "dialects", something "less than a real language". And in folk-linguistic prescriptivist thought, words and expressions which do not comply to norms and standards are not "real", they "don't exist".

Bengt Pohjanen has expressed this beautifully in his autobiographic novel *Jopparikuninkhaan poika* ('The son of the smuggler king'). His language is Meänkieli (aka Tornedal Finnish), a Northern Finnish variety spoken by an autochthonous minority in the Swedish far north and officially acknowledged as a minority language in Sweden since 2000. Meänkieli, although traditionally considered a dialect of Finnish, clearly deviates from those modern Finland Finnish varieties which since the 1960s–70s have been spoken by hundreds of thousands of Finnish immigrants and their descendants in the industrial centres of Central and Southern Sweden (such as Södertälje or Torslanda in Gothenburg, mentioned in the following quotation).

> *Ennää mie en halvaa olla viehraana toisten toelisuuessa. Mie hääyn oppia suomen, niin, sitä suomea, jota met puhuma ja jota ei vielä ole olemassa, mutta jota mie kannan syämessä sikiönnä, joka jo kauon oon oottanu minun hajoaamista ja sen syntymistä. Enhään mie*

sitä vielä käsitä, ette mie halvaan synnyttää minun äitinkielen. Samaan se sille, ette mie olen keskonen, mutta minun kielen synnyttäjä mie halvaan olla itte. En mie äpärää halvaa synnyttää rääkhyyn Södertälhjeen Scaniafapriikin krinnuitten ulkopuolele, enkä mie halvaa minun sikiötä huuthaan Torslandavärkissä kilpaa konheitten kans, ette hän halvaa syntyä häänki. Minun kieli halvaa ulos niinku kaikki kielet halvaava, syyreä saahmaan, henkhiin ja haisthaan, anthaan kukile nimiä, kaloile kans, selithään juttuja ja tinkaahmaan, lauhlaan ja itkheen, olheen muitten kielten roikassa. Mie halvaan synnyttää kielen ja sitte auttaa muitaki synnythään. Mie halvan kielen paanmuskaksi.
(Pohjanen 2009, 190–191)

'I don't want to be a guest in the reality of others[24] any more. I must learn Finnish, yes, the kind of Finnish that we speak, the language which doesn't exist yet but which I'm carrying in my heart like a child that has long waited for me to go into labour and give birth to it. I don't understand yet that I want to give birth to my mother tongue. Never mind that I was prematurely born, I myself want to be the one who gives birth to my language. I don't want to have a bastard who cries outside the gates of the Scania factory in Södertälje, and I don't want my child to yell through the noise of the machines in the factory in Torslanda, telling me that he, too, wants to be born. My language wants to come out like all languages do, to get oxygen, to breathe and to smell, to give names to flowers, and to fish, too, to explain things and to barter, to sing and to cry, to be a language among other languages. I want to give birth to the language and then help others give birth, too. I want to be the midwife of language.'
(transl. by J.L.)

24. *"Guest in the reality"* is an allusion to the title of Pär Lagerkvist's famous novel Gäst hos verkligheten from 1925, a story of a young boy's religious and philosophical search for the meaning of life and death.

Pohjanen's midwife metaphor provides a skilful way of combining the two dimensions of language, "nature" or spontaneous pre-existence and "nurture" or conscious human agency, or bridging the gap between the ethnolinguistic assumption (the idea that there is a simple one-to-one correspondence between a monolingual and monocultural individual's ethnic identity and language, an organic connection as between a mother and her child; see e.g. Blommaert et al. 2012, 4) and the standard-language ideology which claims that not even native speakers can truly possess or master their language without formal education (Milroy 2001, 537); that is, metaphorically, without the help of a trained and licensed midwife. At the same time, it hides or naturalizes the social dimension of language in the sense of interpersonal conventions: for Pohjanen, language is first of all his and then each individual's own child. What, in this case, is authentic, what is constructed? This question, the legitimacy of language planning based on its authenticity, has arisen in the history of the Finno-Ugric state languages as well[25]: is this the (authentic) language of the people or a (planned) language for the people? But for the non-state languages, due to the special position of literature in their maintenance, this question is especially connected to literature.

25. For Finnish and Estonian, see especially Laakso 2018.

2. Multilingualism of minorities, conventions of literature

Today's speakers of Finno-Ugric minority languages are all bilingual or multilingual: they master the dominant majority language, especially in written and formal registers often even more fluently and more confidently than their own heritage language. The majority language is almost inevitably present in their everyday life, at their workplaces, in public services and mass media, in the education system and in communication with majority-language speakers who often do not understand the minority language and sometimes don't even tolerate its use in their presence. And even in in-group use, even the most conservative minority language speakers' language use is often characterized by frequent code-switching, code-mixing, and nonce loans.

Multilingualism thus belongs to the everyday life of minority-language speakers. However, multilingualism also clearly deviates from the ideals of national language planning. In the tradition of language planning and language-related symbol politics established in most European nation states, a unified national language was seen as a symbol of national unity, and, correspondingly, an ideal language would display minimal variation in form and a high degree of stability (see e.g. Haugen 1966, 931). Moreover, this tradition often includes purism, an avoidance of conspicuously foreign elements which may represent the history of foreign oppression and underline the subordinated character of the minority language ("they don't even have a word of their own for X"). For this reason, "minority language communities often face contentious debate over whether the language can survive without foreign borrowings and whether it loses its cultural value with too many foreign words" (Garland 2008, 115).

Conspiring with monolingual ("homogenizing") conventions and practices of literature, monolingual standard-language ideologies will inevitably clash with the multilingual reality of today's minorities and the requirement of authenticity or "linguistic realism" (Cagnoli 2010). And paradoxically, of minority and migrant literature, multilingualism and explicit representations of it (from the perspective of the majority) are also often expected (cf. Tidigs 2014, 84; with further references). In the spirit of the ethnolinguistic assumption, minority literature is supposed to represent the essentialized minority's mentality, world view, and culture in the same way as the traditional role of female authors was to describe women's world, woman's psyche or the feminine world view (for a generic male reader). Both in linguistics and in literature studies, minority authors' multilingualism has often been received as a truthful representation of the multilingual world in which the authors or their ethnic communities live, or simply as an illustration of the author's individual multilingualism (cf. Tidigs 2014, 89).

Moreover, endangerment and the pressure of the dominant language make speakers of minority languages often extremely language-conscious, to the point that conversations *in* an endangered language tend to turn into conversations *about* the language (Tsitsipis 1989). Similarly, authors who write *in* an endangered language may end up writing *about* the endangered language: they have an explicit emancipatory agenda which includes consciousness-raising about language-related problems. These problems, in turn, include multilingual issues such as the question of "foreign words", language issues in the education system, or communication problems with the majority people. In the above-mentioned novel *Jopparikuninkhaan poika,* these language issues surface, on every second or third page at least. The following example illustrates a very typical traumatic situation at school, in the author's childhood in the 1940s–50s when many children still entered the monolingual Swedish school system as monolingual Meänkieli speakers:

> *Meilä oon psalmvärsyjä ollu läksynä. "Det är en ros utsprungen, av Jesse rot och stam, av Fadren är upprunnen till evig salighet." Kalle pinnistää pölöstä naama punasenna ja opettaja tietenki havattee sen ja käskee Kallen lukea psalmvärsyn. Kalle freistaa. Mie viskuttelen sille. Jessen ruusu mennee hyvin, Jesse James oon tuttu värkki, niin juuri ja runko, net oon olemassa Kallen mailmassa, mutta "Fadren" joka oon "upprunnen"? Kalle vahtaa minua avuton ilme kasuvilla. "Auta, Pänktti-rukka." Mie viskuttelen kämmenen kalhveessa ja Kallen ilme kirkastuu ko se lukkee juhlalisesti: "Och Fadren är i brunnen i evig salighet!" Ei se saattanu muuale Fadrea panna ko kaihvoon. Piru oon taas irti. Kaikin ulvova ja klaakottavva. Kalle ei ossaa ruottia!* (Pohjanen 2009, 153)
>
> 'We have got a home assignment to learn some hymn verses. *Det är en ros utsprungen, av Jesse rot och stam, av Fadren är upprunnen till evig salighet* ['A rose has sprung up from Jesse's root and stem, from the Father has arisen to eternal bliss']. Kalle is struggling, his face red with anguish, and the teacher of course notices it and tells Kalle to read the verse aloud. Kalle is trying hard. I'm whispering to him. Jesse's rose is OK, we know Jesse James, and roots and stems, they exist in Kalle's world, but what's that "Fadren" who is "upprunnen"? Kalle stares at

> me with a helpless expression on his face. "Help me, Pänktti, please!" I whisper behind my palm, and Kalle's face lights up as he reads solemnly: "Och Fadren är i brunnen i evig salighet!" ['And the Father is in the well in eternal bliss!'] He just couldn't place "Fadren" anywhere else but into the well. Hell is loose again. Everybody is howling with laughter. Kalle doesn't know Swedish!' (transl. by J.L.)

The requirement for "documentary" realism (also at the service of ethnolinguistic emancipation, for example, pointing out the traumatic consequences of linguistic oppression, as in the previous example) can be fulfilled in two ways. The monolingual strategy means restricting the themes, topoi, and genres to exclude all contexts in which the dominant language must be present, such as modern urban life or interactions with authorities. This may lead to ethnographic or historical descriptions of traditional communities (cf. Cagnoli 2010 for Komi) or to focusing on specific genres such as historical fiction or lyric poetry – as in the Finland Swedish literature, which often has chosen this strategy to avoid what Clas Zilliacus calls the "reality police" (Zilliacus 2002, quoted in Tidigs 2014, 22).

In many cases, however, the expectations of minority literature make the representation of the majority language in narration or dialogue inevitable. In what follows, I will attempt a brief survey of the forms in which this multilingualism appears. Before that, however, some basic concepts and approaches to the research of literary multilingualism must be presented.

3. Code-switching vs. literary multilingualism

In the research of literary multilingualism, the forms and strategies of literary code-switching, insertion of foreign elements, or other means of making other languages present in the text have been investigated with very diverse tools, using different typologies and terminologies.

Some linguists have attempted to apply the theories and research methods from spoken code-switching to literary multilingualism as well; for example, Callahan (2004) has investigated Spanish-English written code-switching using Myers-Scotton's Matrix

Language Frame model, while Laanekask (2002/2003) has applied the same model to German-Estonian bilingualism in the letters of 19th-century Estonian activists of the national awakening. In its purest form, this means focusing on grammar and the structural properties of the texts as a written representation of spoken discourse, and is, of course, burdened with all the problems of these somewhat Procrustean models. Namely: the role of universal structural constraints for code-switching has been questioned. Indeed, counter-examples can be found to practically any purportedly universal constraint, which has led, for example, Verschik (2004) to conclude that an exclusively structural-linguistic approach to code-switching cannot be productive and that research should also pay attention to sociolinguistic and attitudinal factors.

At the same time, the concept of code-switching itself is controversial and debated. This criticism is connected with the ideas that languages themselves are merely social constructs and their borders are nationalist or colonialist artefacts (cf. Makoni and Pennycook 2007; Ansaldo 2010), produced by language policies by way of "atomization of speech forms" (Antia 2015, 479), and that multilingual language users are not switching between completely distinct, different systems but rather "polylanguaging" (see e.g. Jørgensen 2008; Jørgensen et al. 2011; Antia 2015), drawing on their coexisting and intertwined linguistic repertoires (Sarhimaa 1999, 306–307), employing "whatever linguistic features are at their disposal with the intention of achieving their communicative aims" (Jørgensen 2008, 169–170), or "simply communicating in patterns that [are] familiar to them" (Garner 2004, 212). (In fact, both in cases of closely related languages – such as former dialects or patois varieties which are now emancipating themselves as independent literary languages closely related to the dominant language – and with minority languages which are already marked by centuries-old contacts with the dominant language so that lexical items and even phonological or morphosyntactic features have been taken over, the border between code-switching and adapted old loanwords or normal language use and specifically mixed lects is difficult to determine.)

In this view, what is really interesting about multilingualism in literature is not the rules by which the "languages" alternate in the text but how both or all of them are used for "the reflection, construction and reconstruction of a hybrid/third space identity, which is fluid and always in transition" (Jonsson 2005, 254). That is, the interest is in a "linguistically hybrid culture" (cf. Sebba 2012, 6), the multilingual identity of the authors and their target audience and the means by which these multilingual or hybrid identities are constructed in the text. There is, however, an in-built controversy in this approach: the concept of hybridity in itself presupposes some kind of distinction between its originally discrete components, and in practice, even researchers who want to distance themselves from the idea of languages as distinct codes cannot investigate multilingualism without the operational concept of languages as systems or even essentialized metaphorical "beings" engaged in interaction or "playing with each other".

> *Kod och kodväxling är andra termer som fortfarande är i flitigt bruk i beskrivningen av litterär flerspråkighet, men som jag har valt att inte använda mig av eftersom en syn på språk som kod har blivit alltmer problematisk att omfatta, särskilt i förhållande till Diktonius.*
> (Tidigs 2014, 31)
>
> '*Code* and *code-switching* are further terms which are still frequently used in the description of literary multilingualism but which I have chosen not to use, because the idea of language as a code has become increasingly problematic to adopt, especially in relation with Diktonius.'
> (transl. by J.L.)
>
> *Det som Diktonius kommentarer kring (åtminstone för vissa läsare, om inte för honom själv) främmande ord visar är just hur glossering inte bara är en översättning från ett språk till ett annat, utan hur det är ett spel mellan språk, där språken kommenterar varandra på olika sätt.*
> (Tidigs 2014, 286)

> 'What Diktonius's comments on certain foreign words (foreign at least for certain readers, if not for himself) show is precisely how glossing is not just translating from a language to another but how it constitutes a game *between* languages, in which languages comment on each other in different ways.'
> (transl. by J.L.)

In any case, even if literary multilingualism may include realistic descriptions of spoken code-switching or code-mixing (as in dialogues), that is, purportedly realistic representations of the multilingual reality in which multilingual authors live, it is inevitably more than just a one-to-one transposition of spoken multilingual discourse to the written medium. Of course, using another language in a literary text is a political act (cf. Jonsson 2012, 215), always related to the prevailing linguistic culture, language policies and literacy practices, the social meanings which the author and the targeted readership assign to the written representations of each language. More importantly, however, using different languages in literature is a poetic act, an issue of choices between different poetic and mimetic strategies in the setting of prevailing literary practices and conventions.

4. Mimetic representations of multilingualism in literature: "echoes of another language"?

In 1981, Meir Sternberg introduced a system for describing the presence of multilingualism in the text by way of four main types of translational mimesis. As Londen (1989, 145; see also Sternberg 1981, 232) has pointed out, these can actually be ordered on a continuum from homogeneous medium (pure monolingualism) to heterogeneous medium.

Starting at the homogeneous (monolingual) end of the continuum, it is possible to completely eliminate all other languages and place the narration and the dialogues into a monolingual world. This can be done by way of *referential restriction*, that is, selecting the topics, settings, and characters so that no other language need be visibly represented, as in countless works of majority literatures in which only the majority language is spoken and used. For minority literatures, as already mentioned, considering both the multilingual reality in which most modern minorities live and the typically emancipatory agenda of minority literatures which implies a focus on language issues, this may be problematic.

Alternatively, the text may be transposed to a monolingual world by way of *homogenizing convention*: only one language is used, and the reader will understand that in the fictive world behind the text, parts of the dialogue or other elements are in another language but that in the text itself, they have all been translated into the medium language. This strategy may come with *explicit attribution,* that is, the presence of another language is explicitly stated – but often this is not necessary: in the reality of many minorities, language choices in certain domains are self-evident. In the following Kven example, for instance, it goes without saying that the news headline has been translated from Norwegian into Kven (which at the time of World War II had no public written use at all):

> *Aviisista taas ihminen oli saannu lukkeet tyskän voittorikhaasta armejasta, joka vain voitti vielä tappaissaki. »Stalingrad valloitettu», oli joku norjan aviisi kirjoittannu, vaikka kaupunki oliki jo ryssän hallussa.*
> (Nilsen-Børsskog 2004, 21)
>
> 'In the newspapers, one could have read about the victorious German army which kept conquering even while losing. "Stalingrad conquered" had stood in some Norwegian newspaper, although the city was already under Russian control.'
> (transl. by J.L.)

From an empirical linguist's point of view, the most problematic point on this scale is the strategy which Sternberg calls *conceptual reflection,* that is, producing "the impression of heterolingualism through culturally typical (or typified) topics, interests, attitudes, realia, forms of address, fields of allusion, or paralinguistic features like gesticulation" (Sternberg 1981, 230–231; Sternberg's own examples include the Philistines' use of the plural form *Elohim* 'gods' in II Samuel 4,8 and the numerous expressions for consecrated oil which a half-Russian character in Rebecca West's *The Birds Fall Down* lists, demonstrating her Orthodox background). The question is whether *culture* and *language* can be conflated and whether expressions associated with a certain cultural or ethnic community can be considered representative of a certain *language*. In literature and cultural studies, there seems to be a temptation to use the concept of *language* as a label for identities, ethnocultural affiliations or aspirations, or language-related emotions and attitudes, something in which lay people typically see an essential connection to language (cf. Laakso 2015). But can we speak of the presence or an "echo" of another language (cf. Wirth-Nesher 2006, 6 about the "echoes" of Yiddish or Hebrew "haunting the text" in Jewish authors' works, quoted in Tidigs 2014, 52) if there are no overtly foreign, linguistically analysable elements or structures, if these "echoes" cannot be subjected to proper linguistic analysis? Doesn't this simply mean that rather than analysing and explaining readers' folk-linguistic intuitions and expectations concerning such texts, scholars are merely sharing them? And even if the presence of the other language is only realized in very fine nuances (for instance, giving the impression of "translated language"), slight statistical deviances in frequencies or collocations, the lack or statistically less prominent use of certain elements or grammatical constructions, etc., wouldn't this rather belong to the "interference" phenomena mentioned under the following point?

5. Explicit multilingual representations of multilingualism: heterogeneous medium

The presence of the other language can be indicated by what Sternberg calls *verbal transposition,* i.e. with "interference": orthographic or phonetic idiosyncrasies, grammatical or stylistic deviances. A very typical means of verbal transposition is the orthographic rendering of foreign accents, but grammatical or even lexical deviances can occur as well.

In practice, *verbal transposition* often co-occurs with the following stage, *selective reproduction.* This means the explicit presence of the other language in the form of a few selected elements. For instance, a character in the story is understood to speak another language, but only a few characteristic words (often: ritualized phrases, address words, expressions for ethnographically interesting or characteristic phenomena) are given in this original language, the rest is translated into the medium language. In practice, they may also co-occur with interference features. The selected foreign elements can be left untranslated, but an additional translation can also be given, as in this example from Alf Nilsen-Børsskog's novel. The Kven protagonists are hiding from the German occupying army; when they are running out of food supplies, they meet a friendly Saami reindeer herder who can sell them some reindeer meat. Actually, the novel describes many encounters with the Saami, and the narrator often explicitly mentions that many Kven also knew Saami and both languages were used in interethnic communication.

> *Taas tuli täysi hiljaisuus. Pitkä hiljaisuus. Sitte väärtti selhäätti kurkkuu monta kerttaa. «Naa, go nu lea,» ko se pojat niin on, sanoi poromies, ko hän oli tutkiskellu asiaa pitkän aijan, «naa, myyn mie teile rahattaki. Aika on semmoinen, ette tarvittee auttaat toista hädässä.»*
> (Nilsen-Børsskog 2004, 388)
>
> 'A complete silence ensued again. A long silence. Then the Saami friend cleared his throat many times. *"Naa, go nu lea,"* ['well, if it is so'] if it's so, boys, said the reindeer herder after thinking about it for a long time, "well, I'll sell it to you even without money. These are such times that one must help another in need.'
> (transl. by J.L.)

Both interference features and selective reproduction set certain requirements to the readership: readers should be able to recognize the "foreign" features and usually also assign them to a certain language variety. In other words, the readership is expected to share the author's linguistic or folk-linguistic knowledge about those certain strange or funny ways of speaking which are supposed to characterize a certain group or kind of speakers or even act as shibboleths "giving away" the speakers' foreign origin.

Interference features may also represent a fictive, generic "foreign accent" or folk-linguistic but linguistically incorrect general beliefs about another language, that is, a mock ethnolect (as in North American "Mock Spanish" in which an *o* is added to English words – *no problemo!* – or in Finnish "Mock Estonian" in which Finnish voiceless stops are substituted with *b d g* also in linguistically incorrect ways). Misinterpreted or non-existent linguistic features are used to create "foreignness" in the following example from Ortjo Stepanov's novel *Kotikunnan tarina* ('Story of my kinsfolk'). The novel, published in Soviet Karelia in 1979, describes life in a White Sea Karelian village from the 1920s to World War II. The medium of narration is Standard Finnish, which for White Sea Karelian authors of Stepanov's generation was the standard language: they had been taught to regard their Karelian as a dialect of Finnish. In the dialogue, however, the Karelian characters speak mostly Karelian and only switch to Finnish in more formal contexts or with ethnic Finnish interlocutors, as in this example. At a logging site in the forest Sakun Jaakko, a local Karelian, is chatting with the foreman Kalle Lahti, one of those "Red" Finns who escaped to the Soviet Union after the civil war of 1918.

> *– Juu, juu. Kuulemma rajan takaa on tuotu hevosia.*
> *– Jottako?! Jaakko ihan ponnahti pystyyn.*
> *– Niin rahatimiehet kertoivat.*
> *»Rahatimies» samoin kuin monissa muissa sanoissa Kalle äännähti kerakkeiden väliin liian ääntiön mikä synnytti lisätavuja ja teki lausunnan jotenkin katkonaiseksi.*
> (Stepanov 1979, 25)
>
> '– Yeah, yeah. They say that horses have been imported from across the border.
> – Really?! Jaakko literally jumped up.
> – That's what the freight wagon drivers told me.

> In the word »rahatimies» [i.e. *rahtimies* 'freight wagon driver'] as in many other words Kalle pronounced a superfluous vowel between the consonants, which created additional syllables and made his speech somewhat choppy.'
> (transl. by J.L.)

Although old-school Soviet White Sea Karelian authors like Stepanov had acquired an excellent command of Standard Finnish in their education, also thanks to the very close relatedness between Finnish and their White Sea Karelian native dialect, this attempt to imitate dialectal spoken Finnish is linguistically incorrect. Epenthetic vowels do appear in some stem-internal consonant clusters in many Finnish dialects (e.g. *vahava* instead of *vahva* 'strong'), but never between *h* and *t*. However, for the author's purposes this incorrect imitation or "Mock Dialectal Finnish" does the job: it marks the presence of a substandard variety and, in a way, positions this speaker – despite his superior position at the logging site and his wartime merits – on the same level of authenticity and solidarity with uneducated Karelians whose speech also deviates from Standard Finnish.

In principle, it is also possible to make the text truly multilingual, with ample switches between languages. This may represent real-life multilingual discourses, either realistically – for instance, bilingual characters in their dialogue switch freely between their languages – or by way of *vehicular matching* (Sternberg 1981, 223–224), assigning to each language a certain vehicular role or function in the text. A kind of vehicular matching is traditionally used in realistic prose where the narration is in the standard language but the dialogue of dialect speakers represents their dialect(s). This appears in the works of Ortjo Stepanov and other White Sea Karelian authors of his generation as well: Karelians in their traditional community speak Karelian, while the narration is in Standard Finnish.

In many minority literatures, the switches will operate in the other direction. The majority language can be freely used in dialogues, or in realistic representations of the presence of the majority language as the prospective readership is bilingual and will understand all majority-language items without any difficulties. The use of the majority language in the dialogue can add a realistic touch to the text for readers in whose everyday life the use of their minority language in certain domains is out of question. In this example from a Mari-language short story by V. Berdinskij (published in 2010, quoted from Gavrilova 2013, 34), Soviet officers simply cannot speak Mari, the language of the narration, as Mari never was officially used in the Russian or the Soviet army. The requirement of sociolinguistic authenticity overrides any homogenizing convention or any language-political goal.

> *– Откатить пушки налево!*
> *– Товарищ капитан, надо стрелять, – ӧршдымӧ лейтенант тудын ваштареш лие, – раздавят!*
> *– Слушай приказ: немедленно поверните пушки налево и вон туда, в то логово, понял, сопляк!*
>
> '– Move the cannons to the left!
> – Comrade captain, we must fire, – the clean-shaven lieutenant objected [only this five-word phrase is in Mari], – they'll crush us!
> – This is an order: quickly turn the cannons to the left and over there, towards that hole, d'you understand, you snot-nose!'
> (transl. by J.L.)

Realistic switches to the majority language in the dialogue can also be used to construct the characters by showing their language preferences. A recurring character in minority-language literatures seems to be the "renegade", a person who is a member of the minority speech community in a sense but nevertheless ostentatiously chooses to speak the dominant language, and the overt representation of this language choice serves to express this person's attitudes towards the language and the ethnic identity it represents.

The following example comes from the year 1988, the time of South Estonian (Võro-Seto) ethnolinguistic awakening and the political awakening in Estonia that anticipated the collapse of the Soviet system. These two processes intertwine in the short story *Maas'kamaa* ('Strawberry land') by Kauksi Ülle. The protagonist Liivi, a young teacher, is spending the summer in the South Estonian countryside at her grandmother's, together with her little daughter, while her husband, among other Estonian conscripts in the Soviet army, has been sent to clean up the nuclear catastrophe site in Chernobyl. A silent tension develops between Liivi's family and the neighbour's Russian (!) summer tenants who just don't understand that the local people don't want them to pick "their" wild strawberries near their houses. In this conflict between basically well-meaning but ignorant and nonchalant outsiders on the one side and the South Estonian protagonists on the other, Liivi's mother, a former teacher who is now an invalid after having a nervous breakdown, assumes the role of the renegade both politically and linguistically. Her sympathy with Russians, the Russian language and the Soviet system is in line with her antipathy against the Võro language – which is spoken by all other family members and is also the language of the narration – and consequently, she speaks Standard Estonian.

> *«Vanaimä, aga nä tulõva jo nigu sakslasõ, püssägä!» ütel Liivi. «Vai nä kiäki targõmba ommava,» hiitse vanaimä käega. «Tulliva sakslasõ neläkümne edimädse aasta, nõudsiva spekk ja aier. Neläkümne nelädä tulliva säntesama, küsseva mjässo ja jaitsa. Ütesugudse mõtsalise olliva mõlõmba, ku kõikõ är es anna, käändseva sahvri paheldõ. Anna sis latsilõ midä tahat.»*
> *«Mida sa lastele õpetad?» kärät imä vanaimäle pääle. Imä ol' noorõlt inne ku segi lät's pioneerijuht olnu ja parteilane päälekauba, ku tä vihalõ lät's, nakas alati rääkmä. «Mis siis sellest, et meil Leningradist suvitajad on, õpitegi vene keele selgeks.»*
> *«Sa vast tahat, et Mari nakkaski sullõ baabuška ütlemä,» naarsõ Liivi.*
> *«Kuidas sa räägid emaga! Mida sa koolis lastele õpetama hakkad!» – «Kuis midä, eesti kiilt oppa.»*
> (Kauksi Ülle 1988, 24)

"Grandma, they are coming just like the Germans did, with guns!", Liivi said. "As if one were wiser than another," Grandma shrugged. "The Germans came in '41, required *Speck* and *Eier* ['bacon and eggs']. In '44, these came in the same way, asking for *myaso* and *yaytsa* ['meat and eggs']. Wild beasts all the same, if you didn't give them all you had, they would turn your larder upside down. Then you can give your children whatever you please."
"*What are you teaching to the children?"* Mommy snapped to Grandma. In her youth, before she went nuts, Mommy had been a leader in the Pioneers [Communist children's organisation] and even a member of the Party. When she got roused, she always started speaking [i.e. Standard Estonian; the verb *rääkmä,* Standard Estonian *rääkima* 'speak', instead of typically and indexically South Estonian *kõnõlõma,* indicates the language]. *"What's wrong with the summer tenants coming to us from Leningrad? You will learn proper Russian."*
"Do you want Mari to start calling you *babushka*?" Liivi laughed.
"How are you talking to your mother? What are you going to teach to the children at school?" –
"Depends. I'll teach them Estonian."
(transl. by J.L.; Liivi's mother's lines in Standard Estonian italicized by J.L.)

Outside the dialogue and the issues of people's language choices, the use of the majority language may simply be due to the requirement of linguistic realism. For instance, the minority language is often never represented in public signage.

Кӧзяин пуктiс пызан вылӧ кык книга, кодъясӧс видзис шкапас. Ӧтиас пасйысьӧны локтысь-мунысьяс, почта да эстафета. Мӧдыслы мышкас гижӧма рочӧн: »Для жалоб».
(Fedorov 1982, 9)

'The landlord brought two books which he kept in his cupboard and put them on the table. Into

> one of them, travellers, postmen and message-bearers wrote their names. On the spine of the other, there stood in Russian: »Dlya zhalob ['For complaints']».'
> (transl. by J.L.)

This example, in Komi, comes from a historical novel about the life of Ivan A. Kuratov, the pioneer of Komi literature. In this scene, the young Kuratov, on his way home from the priest seminar in Vologda, is stopping at a postal station, where he has to show his passport and sign the guestbook. This takes place in 1861, at a time when the Komi language was practically never used in writing and had no official status whatsoever, and for official and semi-official public signage and the like, Russian was the only thinkable option in these parts of the Russian empire. The text "For complaints" just couldn't be in any other language, certainly not in Komi, and considering that practically all Komi speakers today are bilingual in Russian, any prospective reader will recognize and understand the Russian words without any explanations. However, for some reason the author wants to explicitly comment on the language – perhaps in order to apologize for the breach against the homogenizing convention, as the narration otherwise is consistently in Komi.

And the story goes on. On the following page, Kuratov after signing in starts looking around in the room and notices some pictures on the wall. (His reaction serves to construct the Soviet-time "official" image – somewhat counterfactual, in fact, cf. Bartens 1990 – of Kuratov, the national poet, as a critic of religion and the Orthodox church, despite his clerical education.)

> *Куратов сюсьджыка видзӧдліс ен нога картинаяс вылӧ. Ӧти вылын Георгий победоносец вӧв вылын пукалӧ, кузь шыӧн зургӧ веглясьысь змейлы. Уліас гижӧд: »Как Егорий во бою на серу сидит коню, держит в руце копие, тычет змию в жопие...»*
> *Куратов эз вермы кутчысьны да вак-вакӧн серӧктіс, быттьӧ пес чипас гольдіс-киссис.*
> (Fedorov 1982, 10)

> 'Kuratov took a closer look at the pictures which resembled icons. On one of them, St. George was sitting on a horse, piercing the crawling dragon with a long spear. Below him, the text: »Kak Egoriy [...]» ['How George in the battle sitteth on a grey horse, holdeth a spear in his hand, poketh the dragon's arse...']
> Kuratov couldn't restrain himself but burst into a rumbling laughter, as if a stack of firewood were falling down.'
> (transl. by J.L.)

The text in what turns out to be a parody or a caricature of an Orthodox icon is in archaizing language, a parody of Church Slavonic in fact, and represents a genre and a register for which there is no equivalent in Komi – after the mediaeval Old Permic literacy had been given up, in Kuratov's times the Russian Orthodox church only used Church Slavonic or Russian, and any parodic puns at the cost of religious language could only function in these languages. Consequently, the homogenizing convention simply cannot be applied. What we see here is vehicular matching conditioned by style or register in a multilingual setting, for readers whose bilingualism enables code-switching for stylistic purposes.

Beyond vehicular matching, multilingualism can form an essential part of the dialogue or even the narration. These multilingual texts invite the reader to share the aesthetic, emotional and intellectual joys of crossing the language border, using "multilayered" (Verschik 2013, 23) multilingual puns or playing on culture-specific meanings, semantic nuances or connotations which only readers who know both or all the languages involved can understand. Macaronic texts challenge their readers to creatively and consciously use their full linguistic repertoire and (folk-)linguistic knowledge of the languages involved: they stimulate (and require) language awareness and direct the reader's attention from the message to the medium. They are often "inside jokes", targeting an academic, educated readership (as in classical European macaronic poetry which operates with Latin and local vernaculars) or fellow members of a multilingual community in which multilingualism is perceived as socially indexical, characteristic of "us". Macaronic folklore often arises in multilingual contexts, as in the Estonian-Russian-German trilingual urban speech communities in Estonia before World War I:

> *Eines Tages tahtsin minna*
> *üle silla встретиться,*
> *aber kui ma jõudsin sinna,*
> *kam die Mutter luuaga.*
> (Ariste 1981)
>
> '[German:] One day [Estonian:] I wanted to go across the bridge [Russian:] for a rendez-vous, [German:] but [Estonian:] as I got there, [German:] the mother came [Estonian:] with a broomstick.'
> (transl. by J.L.)

Interestingly, however, true macaronic texts in which "polylingual means are [...] flagrantly summoned to represent a unilingual reality of discourse" (Sternberg 1981, 224) are hard to find in the young written literatures of the Finno-Ugric minorities. Instead of "vehicular promiscuity", a term which Tidigs (2014, 52) criticizes with good reason, it seems that either the homogenizing convention or vehicular matching in the spirit of linguistic realism is the preferred strategy.

Although the Sternbergian continuum from monolingual to multilingual medium offers a nice approach to the classification of the different forms of literary multilingualism, it has some problematic points, most notably the idea of "conceptual reflection", that is, "multilingualism within one language". As Tidigs (l.cit.) points out, Sternberg doesn't seem to really understand the legitimacy of literary multilingualism outside mere depiction of reality (which, for most modern minorities, is multilingual anyway), that is, the poetic function of multilingualism. Furthermore, the dimension of monolingual vs. multilingual medium doesn't essentially help in understanding the poetic or political functions of literary multilingualism. The question is rather *how* real-life multilingualism – because the real-life language use of modern minorities is multilingual in any case – is translated into the mostly monolingual conventions and ideals of literature and language planning and what this means for the literature and the language for which minority-language authors inevitably carry a burden of responsibility and moral obligations. This, finally, brings us to the issues of authenticity and emancipation.

6. Authenticity and emancipation: returning to where we started

Minority literatures draw their political legitimation from the authenticity of the language whose "birth" they assist, as in Bengt Pohjanen's midwife metaphor cited above: the language has the right to be born because it actually exists already and wants to be born. Authenticity, a much-discussed concept in sociolinguistics, as Coupland (2010, 104) summarizes, is a question of values which are related to ontology (authentic things are "real"), historicity (authentic things are durable or even timeless), systemic coherence (authenticity is seen as a matter of making sense and imposing order) and consensus (social process of authentication). This list can be connected to a corresponding list of folk-linguistic ideas about language (cf. Niedzielski and Preston 1999).

As concerns ontology: in lay people's thought, real languages "exist" as entities in a kind of reality (while incorrect or inferior forms of language "do not exist" – "there's no such word", "it's not a real word"). That is, written and standardized languages, even if their standardized written representations are created with the painstaking work of language activists (the "midwives"), exist for real, while a language without writing is not a real language.

Historicity corresponds to the idea of the authentic language being old, ancient, or original. Folk ideas of certain languages (especially those that are felt to be of particular emotional or nationalist value) being "older" than others are widely spread and difficult to part with. Besides, with many endangered languages the process of language loss is imminent, with the oldest generations being the most fluent speakers, which creates or strengthens the impression that the language as such belongs to the past. Systemic coherence, in turn, can be seen as related to the idea of languages being clear-cut systems with clear borders. And finally, social authentication – the fact that authenticity is negotiated in intersubjective and collective processes – corresponds to the folk idea of an inextricable link between a language and the groupness of its users who will either accept or reject each utterance, expression or text (cf. e.g. Edwards 2009, 55).

Relating these aspects to the dimension of multilingualism vs. homogeneity shows how complicated the idea of authenticity can be for a multilingual speech community. The first three aspects seem to be connected to idealized homogeneity, purity (or purism) and monolingualism. Language planning ("correctness"), idealizing an imagined original monolingualism (for the repercussions of this idea in Finno-Ugric linguistics, see Laakso 2014), and the idea of "languageness" (Garner 2004) or the language existing as a system might all speak in favour of monolingual strategies. However, the social aspects of authentication can also be connected to group multilingualism, celebrating a multilingual group identity (as in the case of macaronic folklore): actually, we are a people of many languages!

This, in fact, is explicitly expressed in Alf Nilsen-Børsskog's historical novel, one of the first works of Kven literature, with obvious emancipatory goals. Here, the author again stages a meeting between his Kven protagonists and their Saami neighbours:

> *Ko poropaimen saattoi norjaa ja omma kieltä ja lisäksi puhui vielä pyssyjokilaistenki kieltä, niin tunturilla pyssyjokilaistelthiin, ja puhuskelthiin vähän paimenen kieltäki. Het olthiin kieltten tunttijoita. [...] Kello oli jo sivvu keskipäivän ennen ko miehet lähđethiin siitä. Het sanothiin «hyvästi» väärttile, jota het tulleissa olthiin puuristelheet. Sehän kuului hyvhiin taphoin. Väärtti huusi vielä heiđän pörhään: «Ampukkaa, pojat, niitä porroi. Siinä on pieni tšorrakka pohjaisemppaa. Net on minun. En mie jätä niitä tyskälaisele. Ja menkkää tervheenä,» lisäis hän vielä omala kielelä. «Jää sieki tervheenä!»*
> (Nilsen-Børsskog 2004, 138)

> 'As the reindeer herder knew Norwegian and his own language and also spoke the language of the Pyssyjoki people, they talked in Pyssyjoki way and also chatted a little in the reindeer herder's language. They were language-savvy people. [...] It was already past noon when the men left. They said "goodbye" to their Saami friend whom they had greeted with *bures* [Saami greeting word] as they came. That belonged to good manners. The Saami friend shouted after them: "Shoot those reindeer, boys. There's a small herd to the North. They belong to me. I'm not going to leave them to the German. And go healthy" [literal translation of the Saami *mannet dearvan* 'goodbye'], he added in his own language. "You stay healthy, too!" (transl. by J.L.)

Now if we look closer at the text, we actually find that it highlights and celebrates and explicitly thematizes multilingualism with very sparse and almost purely monolingual means. Although it is explicitly emphasized that the Saami language was an essential and welcome part of the protagonists' world, the text only has one half-adapted Saami loanword *(tšorrakka),* one adapted derivative of a Saami word *(puuristele-* 'greet with *bures*') and a literal translation of a Saami idiom ('go/stay healthy!'). In other words, the "multilingualism" in this text very much resembles the "multilingualism" of Mikael Niemi's *Populärmusik från Vittula* (cf. Jonsson 2012): there's a lot of talk about the other language while real representations of the language are few and far between, are realized on different levels (more or less adapted loanwords, literal translations etc.) and might even go unnoticed.

This, finally, is why it would be so important and interesting to distinguish the different types of representations of literary multilingualism from each other. Thematization of multilingualism does not require the explicit presence of the other language. The implicit presence of the other language can assume many forms which can often only be understood in connection with the linguistic culture and history of the speech community depicted – in other words, mimetic representations of language-related issues may be at least as challenging to the reader or to the researcher as overt multilingualism. And, furthermore, no single dimension of multilingualism – focusing on the monolingualism or multilingualism of the medium, or the form in which the elements of the other language appear, or on the ideological or stylistic functions of switching and mixing in constructing hybrid identities, or on the roles of different languages – can alone do justice to the diverse forms and uses of multilingualism in literature. Moreover, in order to understand how and why multilingualism and different languages can be represented in literature, we must understand the role of folk-linguistic ideas about language and languages. They condition not only language policy (cf. Albury 2016) but also the use of different languages in literature – recall that literature for many Finno-Ugric minorities is the highest level of official language use they can reach, regulated by language policies of the authorities!

And, finally, why have I chosen to talk about this from the point of view of Finno-Ugric minority languages? These languages and their mostly young literatures have many common features, such as the tradition of nationalist, prescriptive linguistic culture or the emancipatory agenda, which can lead to a focus on either monolingual purity or multilingual realism. However, they exist in very different political and historical frameworks and have hardly ever been investigated from the point of view of multilingualism and in a comparative perspective, especially as concerns the implicit contradiction between what exists – the "authentic" language – and what needs to be created or reproduced, between authenticity and emancipation. In order to really tackle these complicated problems, profound expertise in both linguistics and literature studies would be needed, and an immense amount of work remains to be done.

List of references and sources

Albury, Nathan J. 2016. 'The power of folk linguistic knowledge in language policy.' *Language Policy* 15 (2): 1–20.

Ansaldo, Umberto. 2010. 'Identity alignment and language creation in multilingual communities.' *Language Sciences* 32: 615–623.

Antia, Bassey E. 2015. 'Language policy and terminology in South Africa.' In *Handbook of Terminology*, Vol. 1, edited by Hendrik J. Kockaert and Frieda Steurs, 467–488. Amsterdam.

Ariste, Paul. 1981. *Keelekontaktid. Eesti keele kontakte teiste keeltega.* Tallinn. (=Emakeele Seltsi toimetised, 14).

Bartens, Raija. 1990. 'Kuratovin Jumala-kuva.' In *Komin kansan ensimmäinen runoilija. 150 vuotta I. A. Kuratovin syntymästä*, edited by Johanna Laakso. Helsinki. (=Castrenianumin toimitteita, 36).

Blommaert, Jan, Sirpa Leppänen, and Massimiliano Spotti. 2012. 'Endangering multilingualism.' In *Dangerous Multilingualism: Northern Perspectives on Order, Purity, and Normality*, edited by Jan Blommaert, Sirpa Leppänen, Päivi Pahta and Tiina Räisänen, 1–24. Houndmills.

Cagnoli, Sébastien. 2010. 'Bilingualism in Komi society as reflected in national drama.' (Paper presented at the 11th International Congress for Finno-Ugric Studies at Piliscsaba, Hungary, August 12, 2010).

Callahan, Laura. 2004. *Spanish/English Codeswitching in a Written Corpus*. Amsterdam.

Coupland, Nikolas. 2010. 'The authentic speaker and the speech community.' In *Language and Identities*, edited by Carmen Llamas and Dominic Watts, 99–112. Edinburgh.

Edwards, John. 2009. *Language and Identity: An Introduction*. Cambridge.

Fedorov, Gennadij. 1982. Востым. Сыктывкар.

Garland, Jennifer. 2008. 'The minority language and the cosmopolitan speaker: Ideologies of Irish language learners.' PhD thesis, University of California, Santa Barbara.

Garner, Mark. 2004. *Language: an ecological view*. Bern. (=Contemporary Studies in Descriptive Linguistics, 1).

Gavrilova, Valentina Grigorievna. 2013. 'Переключение кодов в художественной литературе на марийском языке.' *Филология и культура* 31 (1): 30–35. Accessed April 8, 2015. http://cyberleninka.ru/article/n/pereklyuchenie-kodov-v-hudozhestvennoy-literature-na-mariyskom-yazyke.

Haugen, Einar. 1966. 'Language, Dialect, Nation.' *American Anthropologist* 68: 922–935.

Huddart, David. 2008. *Postcolonial theory and autobiography*. Abingdon.

Jonsson, Carla. 2005. 'Code-switching in Chicano Theater: Power, Identity and Style in Three Plays by Cherríe Moraga.' PhD thesis, Umeå University.

– 2012. 'Making silenced voices heard: code-switching in multilingual literary texts in Sweden.' In: *Language Mixing and Code-Switching in Writing. Approaches to Mixed-Language Written Discourse*, edited by Mark Sebba, Shahrzad Mahootian and Carla Jonsson, 212–232. Abingdon.

Jørgensen, J. Norman. 2008. 'Introduction: Polylingual Languaging Around and Among Children and Adolescents.' *International Journal of Multilingualism* 5 (3): 161–176.

Jørgensen, J. Norman, Martha Sif Karrebæk, Lian Malai Madsen, and Janus Spindler Møller. 2011. 'Polylanguaging in Superdiversity.' *Diversities* 13 (2). Accessed February 26, 2017. www.unesco.org/shs/diversities/vol13/issue2/art2.

Kapor, Vladimir. 2009. *Local colour: a travelling concept*. Bern. (=Romanticism and after in France, 13).

Kauksi Ülle. 1988. 'Maas´kamaa.' *Vikerkaar* 8: 20–26.

Kloss, Heinz. 1952. *Die Entwicklung neuer germanischer Kultursprachen von 1800 bis 1950*. München.

Laakso, Johanna. 2014. 'The prehistoric multilingual speaker: what can we know about the multilingualism of Proto-Uralic speakers?' *Finnisch-Ugrische Mitteilungen* 38: 93–114.

– 2015. 'Linguistische und literarische Einblicke. Was uns die Mehrsprachigkeit von der Beziehung von zwei Schwesterwissenschaften lehren kann.' In *Ein Land mit Eigenschaften: Sprache, Literatur und Kultur in Ungarn in transnationalen Kontexten*, edited by Márta Csire, Erika Erlinghagen, Zsuzsa Gáti, Brigitta Pesti and Wolfgang Müller-Funk, 55–66. Wien.

– 2018. 'The language of the people, or a language for the people? On the literarisation of the vernaculars in Finland and Estonia.'

In *Anfangsgeschichten/ Origin Stories: Der Beginn volkssprachiger Schriftlichkeit in komparatistischer Perspektive / The rise of vernacular literacy in a comparative perspective*, edited by Norbert Kössinger, Elke Krotz, Stephan Müller and Pavlina Rychterová. München. (=MittelalterStudien).

Laanekask, Heli. 2002. 'Koodivahetuse grammatikast Koidula kirjades Kreutzwaldile.' In *Lähivertailuja,* Vol. 12, edited by Reet Kasik, 41–56. Tartu. (=Tartu Ülikooli eesti keele õppetooli toimetised, 19).

– 2003. 'Yksi kirjoittaja, monta kieltä: kielenvaihto Lydia Koidulan kirjeissä Friedrich Kreutzwaldille.' In: *Lähivertailuja,* Vol. 11, edited by Ellen Niit and Ulla Palomäki, 47–67. Turku. (=Publications of the Department of Finnish and General Linguistics of the University of Turku, 71).

Lewis, M. Paul, Gary F. Simons, and Charles D. Fennig. 2016. Ethnologue: Languages of the World, Nineteenth edition. Dallas, Texas. Online version: http://www.ethnologue.com.

Londen, Anne-Marie. 1989. *Litterärt talspråk. Studier i Runar Schildts berättarteknik med särskild hänsyn till dialogen.* Helsingfors. (=Skrifter utgivna av Svenska Litteratursällskapet i Finland, 557).

Makoni, Sinfree, and Alastair Pennycook. 2007. 'Disinventing and reconstituting languages.' In *Disinventing and reconstituting languages*, edited by Sinfree Makoni, and Alastair Pennycook, 1–41. Clevedon. (=Bilingual Education and Bilingualism, 62).

Milroy, James. 2001. 'Language ideologies and the consequences of standardization.' *Journal of Sociolinguistics* 5 (4): 530–555.

Niedzielski, Nancy A., and Dennis Preston. 1999. *Folk linguistics.* Berlin.

Nilsen-Børsskog, Alf. 2004. *Kuosuvaaran takana.* S.l.

Pohjanen, Bengt. 2009. *Jopparikuninkhaan poika.* Överkalix.

Sarhimaa, Anneli. 1999. *Syntactic transfer, contact-induced change and the evolution of bilingual mixed codes. Focus on Karelian-Russian language alternation.* Helsinki. (=Studia Fennica Linguistica, 9).

Sebba, Mark. 2012. 'Researching and theorising multilingual texts.' In *Language Mixing and Code-Switching in Writing. Approaches to Mixed-Language Written Discourse*, edited by Mark Sebba, Shahrzad Mahootian, and Carla Jonsson, 1–26. Abingdon.

Stepanov, Ortjo. 1979. *Kotikunnan tarina.* Petroskoi.

Tidigs, Julia. 2014. *Att skriva sig över språkgränserna. Flerspråkighet i Jac. Ahrenbergs och Elmer Diktonius prosa.* Åbo.

Tsitsipis, Lukas D. 1989. 'Skewed performance and full performance.' In: *Investigating obsolescence. Studies in language contraction and death,* edited by Nancy C. Dorian, 117-138. Cambridge. (=Studies in the Social and Cultural Foundations of Language, 7).

Verschik, Anna. 2004. 'Aspects of Russian-Estonian codeswitching: Research perspectives.' *International Journal of Bilingualism* 8 (4): 427–448.

– 2013. 'Mitmekeelsus kui ideaal ja loovuse allikas.' In *Kiili rikkus ja elojoud = Keelte paljusus ja elujõud = Diversity and vitality of languages,* edited by Jüvä Sullõv, 11–29. Võro. (=Publications of Võro Institute, 27).

Wirth-Nesher, Hana. 2006. *Call It English. The Languages of Jewish American Literature.* Princeton.

Zamyatin, Konstantin. 2014. *An Official Status for Minority Languages? A Study of State Languages in Russia's Finno-Ugric Republics.* Helsinki. (=Uralica Helsingiensia, 6).

Zilliacus, Clas. 2002. 'Den finlandssvenska litteraturens korta, lyckliga liv.' In: *On the Threshold. New studies in Nordic literature,* edited by Janet Garton, and Michael Robinson, 62–74. Norwich.

The Voice Crying (or Calling?) in the Wilderness. Possible Similarities between Transylvanism and Meänmaa-Idea

Enikő Molnár Bodrogi

On the title of the paper

The motto of the first document on Transylvanism, a pamphlet written by Károly Kós in 1921, is a quotation from the Bible, John 1,21–23. When I looked up the English version of these verses, I was surprised to learn that they were translated in different ways, the result of different interpretations of the text. I focused on Verse 21, which includes the phrase: "I am the voice of one calling in the wilderness"/ "I am a voice crying in the wilderness"/ "I am the voice shouting in the wilderness" (Bible Hub). It was amazing how well the difference between these translations suits one of the main observations concerning the topic of my research, namely the fact that an ideology can be received in different ways by different minority language groups. The "voice" of an ideologist can either be an echoless cry or a call which the audience answers, depending on the many historical and social circumstances which influence the lives of minorities. The title of this study reflects this recognition. I will come back to this issue later.

1. Introduction

In this research, the term ideology means the system of ideas and beliefs that influence people's choices in their social actions (see Tolcsvai Nagy 2009, 76; Heikkinen 2012, 117).

The present study discusses the following issues: in what historical and social contexts did Transylvanism and the Meänmaa-idea emerge, and what were their aims concerning the reinforcement of the collective identity of the two minorities? I am mainly interested in the cultural and linguistic minority identity implied in the two ideologies.

This study is organized as follows. First, as a historical background to my topic, I briefly present the histories of Transylvania and Meänmaa. Next, I discuss the main features of the two ideologies. Lastly, I summarize the main similarities between the two ideologies as I see them at this stage of my research.

2. A short history of Transylvania

Transylvania (*Erdély* in Hungarian) is situated in the southeastern corner of the Carpathian Basin, and is part of the Romanian territory. During the Middle Ages, it belonged to the Kingdom of Hungary. After the Battle of Mohács in 1526 it became an independent Principality until 1690, when the Habsburgs gained posession of Transylvania through the Hungarian Crown. Transylvania had a separate status within the Habsburg Empire until 1867. After the Austro-Hungarian Compromise of 1867, Transylvania was formally re-annexed to Hungary, as part of the Austro-Hungarian Empire. After World War I, Transylvania was annexed to Romania in the Peace Treaty of Trianon (June 4, 1920) by the victorious Entente Powers. In 1940, Northern

Transylvania was re-annexed by Hungary as a result of the Second Vienna Award and remained part of Hungary until 1944, when the borders of 1920 were re-established. The borders have not been modified ever since (Kocsis and Kocsis-Hodosi 1998, 101–125).

The majority of Hungarians living outside the present-day borders of Hungary live in Romania, mainly in Transylvania. The number of Hungarians in Transylvania was 1,227,623 according to the latest census in 2011 conducted by the National Institute of Statistics in Romania (*Institutul național de statistică* 2011).

Transylvania has had a complex ethno-linguistic, cultural and religious structure, including Romanians (Romanian-speaking ethnic Romanians), Hungarians, Germans, Roma, Ukrainians, and Serbs, amongst others.

3. A short history of Meänmaa

The geographic area called the Torne Valley (*Torniolaakso* in Meänkieli) lies at the border of Finland and Sweden. It was once a culturally and linguistically united area until 1809, when the border between Finland and Sweden was drawn. The Treaty of Hamina (September 17, 1809) ceded almost all the Torne Valley Lappland to Finland. After 1809, the Finnish-speaking people on the western side of the valley became a linguistic minority in Sweden. As a result of the linguistic assimilation policy which started in the 1880s, the language spoken by the Finnish population has become stigmatized and endangered. Most young people of the area have Swedish as their mother tongue. The Finnish dialect spoken on the Swedish side of the Torne Valley, called Meänkieli, was acknowledged as a minority language, in 1999 (Andersson and Kangassalo 2003, 99–108; Arola et al. 2013, 2–3).

The area where Meänkieli (earlier Finnish) is spoken has always been multilingual, with Finnish, Swedish, and Sami being spoken there.

There are no statistics in Sweden concerning the mother tongue of its citizens. The number of the Meänkieli population is estimated to be between 25,000 and 75,000 (Arola et al. 2013, 3; Sulkala 2010, 11; Winsa 2005, 254).

I consider it important to draw a distinction between the names. Torne Valley is a predominantly geographic term, while Meänmaa refers to the specific culture of the area based on Meänkieli, the strongest cultural factor that has characterized the area. The people who speak Meänkieli are most often referred to as Tornedalians, although not all Tornedalians speak or understand Meänkieli any longer.

4. Transylvanism

In the interwar period, Transylvanism has generally been viewed as the main regional ideology of the Transylvanian cultural and spiritual life. It was elaborated by Hungarian writers, historians and journalists in Romania immediately after 1919. However, its roots can be traced back to the Hungarian national movement of the 19th century. Since then, Transylvania has been characterized by multiethnicity and multiculturalism, "democratic Eastern Switzerland" (K. Lengyel 2007, 75–77) and a national supremacy practiced on political level.

This complex ideology aimed to reinforce the collective identity of the ethnic and linguistic minority of Hungarians in Romania who have ever since held onto their own language and cultural heritage.

As some recent research has pointed out, Transylvanism (as regionalism) has not been exclusively a Hungarian brand. There were also Romanian and Saxon[26] Transylvanists, forming their own groups and elaborating their own views upon Transylvania (Török 2007, 128; Nagy 2014, 203).

26. Transylvanian Saxons are the largest and oldest group of the Germans of Romania.

In my study I will focus on the main characteristics of the Transylvanist ideology as elaborated by the Hungarian intellectuals for whom Transylvanism was more predominant than it was for for the Romanians or Germans. It is important to mention that the representatives of Transylvanism have not advocated a well defined or systematic ideology. There are different variants of Transylvanism, which have implied and tolerated contradictory thoughts. Transylvanism was a flexible idea, adjustable to the personal convictions of its representatives (Pomogáts 1983, 8). However, the main issue for them was the political self-determination as an ethno-national entity in Romania and being part of the Hungarian nation culturally.

Transylvanism has mainly been considered a political ideology, but the phenomenon is more than that.

Láng (1998, 5) notes that "Transylvanism is a historical variant of the Hungarian national consciousness".[27] According to Láng, it was meant to give answers to the questions raised by the identity crisis that Hungarians in Transylvania had to encounter in their new, unexpected minority situation. Without political independence and power, the only means of preserving their identity as a community was their own culture, based on national traditions and adjusted to the new situation.

27. In the original: *"A transzilvanizmus a magyarságtudat történelmi változata".*

"Transylvanism was characterized by a strong regional note, linked to the democratic ideal of cultural pluralism" (Török 2003, 128). According to this ideology Transylvania had a specific and particular spirituality which has been shaped throughout the centuries and was rooted in landscape, history, and cultural diversity. Tolerance towards otherness as well as differentness was considered to be the basic feature of this spirituality.

The utopian core of Transylvanism lies in the fact that it postulates a certain historical predestination that all the nations (ethnical groups) in Transylvania could live together in peace and harmony and have equal rights. Károly Kós, the main representative of Transylvanism, believed this to be a reality. Early Transylvanists (such as Károly Kós, Aladár Kuncz) tend to idealize the situation in order to prove the existence of the Transylvanian spirituality or Transylvanian soul (Cs. Gyímesi 1992, 33). In fact, the equal status of all ethnic groups in Transylvania proved to be a utopian dream in the context of the 20th-century nationalism.

The Hungarian minority group began to value the place of birth more than the country they lived in as the basic identity component of the "Hungarian patriot", which lost its validity after the Treaty of Trianon (1920). The political state was based on historical chance, while the birthplace was not, initially, influenced by the change in political power. This is why the birthplace could undertake the identity building role of the homeland.

However, the minority identity did not manifest itself as an ideology, but rather as a collective feeling, in which the earlier national identity could be preserved under a slightly modified form and turn into an ethnic identity. The stability of the natural environment compensated for the fragile and unstable political status.

In the Hungarian literature of this time, Transylvanian nature appears as the bearer of moral values: those of steadiness, loyalty and invincibility (see the poems of László Tompa, Lajos Áprily, Jenő Dsida, Áron Tamási, Mária Berde, Aladár Kuncz).

Transylvanism was seeking the basis of national unity in cultural values, which proved to be more stable than the political criteria. These values had a strong moral charge. A nation was a moral community that manifested itself in its collective culture and demanded from all its members the assumption of a common mission. This messianism constituted one of the central themes of Hungarian literature in Transylvania.

Jenő Dsida, for example, combined in his brilliant poem *Maundy Thursday* a religious topic (the suffering of Jesus in the Garden of Gethsemane) with the topic of the loneliness and spiritual distress of an individual belonging to the Hungarian community in Romania. The parallelism between Jesus and the member of an ethnic minority group is composed tangibly:

> [...]
> it would have been so good to speak a little
> to close friends, a few words to men you trust,
> but there was only damp night, dark and chill,
> Peter was now asleep, and James and John
> asleep, and Matthew, all of them asleep...
> [...]
> (Gömöri 2013)

The ambiguity and the iterative passage between the concrete and the symbolic situation makes the poem so rich in meaning.
In fact Transylvanism was a moral-centered ideology, which holds true also for the Meänmaa-idea, as we will see later in this study.

5. Károly Kós's pamphlet (1921)

Károly Kós (1883–1977), a Hungarian architect, writer, ethnologist and politician, was the most notable advocate of the Transylvanist ideology. He and two contemporary intellectuals of the time, István Zágoni and Árpád Paál, wrote the first document on Transylvanism, a pamphlet entitled *Calling Voice*[28]. They attempted to solve the identity crisis of the Hungarians in Transylvania by introducing the concept of "Transylvanism" and fighting for the territorial autonomy of this ethnic group.

28. It is my conscious choice to use in this case this English translation (and not the *crying/shouting* voice), because Kós's call was received and answered by many Hungarian contemporaries in Transylvania.

The title of the pamphlet refers to an excerpt from the Bible (John 1, 21–23), which serves as the motto for their work:

> *"Akkor megkérdék őtet: Te kicsoda vagy? Ilyés vagy-e te? És monda: nem vagyok. Próféta vagy-e te? És felele: nem vagyok. Mondának azért néki: kicsoda vagy tehát, hogy meg tudjunk azoknak felelni, akik minket elküldöttek; mit mondva magad felől? És monda: Én kiáltó szó vagyok a pusztában!"*
> (Kós 1921).
>
> They asked him, "Then who are you? Are you Elijah?" He said, "I am not." "Are you a Prophet?" He answered, "No." Finally he said, "Who are you? Give us an answer to take back to those who sent us. What do you say about yourself?" John replied in the words of Isaiah the prophet, "I am the voice of one calling in the wilderness."
> (Holy Bible)

In this pamphlet and in his earlier work, such as the weekly review *Kalotaszeg*[29], Kós suggested that there had always existed a particular Transylvanian identity, which had sufficient self-definition and which might offer possibility for the Hungarians in Transylvania to raise this identity to the status of national identity in the context of an ethnic autonomy.

29. *Kalotaszeg*. Képes hetilap. January 7 - March 26, 1912.

> *A régi Magyarország nincs többé számunkra; de Erdély, Ardeal, Siebenbürgen, Transsilvánia, vagy bármi nyelven nevezte és nevezi a világ: feltámadt és van, aminthogy volt akkor is, amikor azt hittük mi magunk, mert azt akartuk hinni, hogy nincs és csak Magyarország van. Akkor is volt, de most is van és akárhogyan is akarja akármilyen akarat, lesz örökön, örökké.*
> (Kós 1921, 2–3)

> 'The former Hungary does not exist any longer for us, but Erdély, Ardeal, Siebenbürgen, Transsilvánia, or in whatever other languages the world has called it, has risen and *exists*, just as it existed when we ourselves believed, *because we wanted to believe*, that it did not exist, only Hungary did. It existed then and it also exists now, and whatever will opposes it in whatever manners, it shall exist forever.'
> (transl. by E.M.B.)

Kós was convinced that the large number of Hungarians in Transylvania guaranteed that they would become an important community in Romania: *"A fundamentum, amire nyugodt lelkiismerettel és bízó lélekkel építhetünk: kétmillió magyar"* 'The basis on which we can build in good conscience and hopeful mind are two million Hungarians' (Kós 1921, 4, transl. by E.M.B.).

Károly Kós believed in the spiritual power of the Hungarians: *"(K)ülön históriai egység ezer esztendő óta, saját, külön erdélyi öntudattal, önálló kultúrával, önérzettel [...]"* '(F)or one thousand years [Transylvania] was an independent historical entity with its own consciousness, independent culture and self-esteem [...]" (Kós 1921, 4, transl. by E.M.B.).

He was definitely demanding "national autonomy" for his ethnic group, seeing it as the only strategy to preserve them from assimilation: *"(M)i, magyar fajú, magyar hitű és magyar nyelvű polgárai Romániának nemzeti autonómiát akarunk, aminek birtokában bennünk Nagy Románia megbízható polgárságot fog nyerni [...]"* '(W)e, citizens of Romania, Hungarians in blood, religion and language, demand national autonomy so that the Greater Romania could gain in us reliable citizens [...]" (Kós 1921, 5, transl. by E.M.B.).

6. The idea of Meänmaa

The idea of Meänmaa has been elaborated by Bengt Pohjanen since the beginning of the 1990s, seventy years later than Transylvanism. Pohjanen (2011a – 2011k) himself has never called it an ideology, rather a philosophy. Pohjanen elaborated his idea in response to the questions raised by the identity crisis he observed in his linguistic minority group, which had become quite visibly assimilated by the Swedish-speaking community. In fact, for those community members who had already undergone language shift, it is natural to use the language with higher prestige in the society. The loss of minority language is not considered a tragedy, because the instrumental function of the language used by members of minorities has proved to be more important than its symbolic function. (See also the case study about the Csángó minority in Romania: Tánczos 2000, 132)

The name Meänmaa, mainly denoting a geographical territory ('our land'), is the name of a country whose inhabitants are connected by their common language (Meänkieli) and culture. This imaginary community is actually a frontier territory not only from a geographical, but also from a cultural, point of view. It belongs neither to the Swedish, nor to the Finnish community; it is an intermediate zone. Tornedalians have been a minority for over two hundred years, since 1809, and the general tendency was to assimilate into the Swedish nation.[30]

30. In my research I have launched the term of Tornedalian ideology, according to which the Tornedalian identity is promoted regardless of the language its representatives use. In spite of some visible similarities between the two ideologies (like the strong link to local nature) Meänmaa-ideology is different because Meänkieli language holds central value in it.

Pohjanen has not elaborated a well-defined or systematic ideology. Nor has he elaborated his Meänmaa-idea in one single work, but in many of his works. The ideology has been based on the need to deconstruct the Swedish nationalistic view of the history of the Torne Valley and its population and to reinforce the identity of his own ethnic and linguistic group.

Pohjanen founded the Meänmaa Association (registered in 2008), whose main goal is the development of a virtual community of all people who have their roots in the Torne Valley and/or who cherish Meänkieli language and culture:

> *Met halvaama koota meänmaalaisia, joita oon pitkin mailmaa ja jokka kerran puhuit yhtä ja sammaa kieltä ja joila olit yhtheiset tavat ja oli yks kansa, jonka tsaarin priimu vuona 1809 jako kahtia Tornionväylää, Muonionväylää ja Könkämäenoa pitkin. […] Se veethiin kysymättä kansalta ja huolimatta siittä, ette se halkasi suvut ja kultturellisen ykseyen.*
> (Meänmaa 2008)

31. I introduce this term to refer to those who once lived in the area of the Torne Valley and who cherish Meänkieli.

'We wish to gather all Meänmaans[31], who live all over the world and who once spoke one and the same language, who had the same habits and were the same nation, whom the line drawn by the Tsaar divided in two in 1809 along the rivers Tornio, Muonio and Könkämä. [...] It [the border] was drawn without asking for the people's permission and without taking into consideration the fact that it split families and a cultural unity.'
(transl. by E.M.B.)

The main features of the Meänmaa-ideology can also be learned from a series of his bilingual feuilletons entitled *The philosophy of Me*änmaa (*Me*änmaas filosofi – Meänmaan filosofii) first published in the trilingual newspaper Haparandabladet – Haaparannanlehti in 2010. Pohjanen accepts the fact that all philosophies and ideologies have their own time and that all nations and groups of people have their own systems of ideas. The most important features of the Meänmaa-philosophy can be summed up as follows:

1. The travel fever. "One of the most specific ideas in Meänmaa has been the philosophy of travelling. People have always set off from here, been in other places and come here from somewhere else"[32] (transl. by E.M.B.).

32. In the original: *"Meänmaan yks ommiimista aatoksista oon reisun filosofii. Täältä oon aina lähetty, muualta oltu ja jostaki tultu"* (Pohjanen 2011a, 72).

2. The syncretism of different political views and orientations (such as "national socialism" and "international socialism"), utopias that emerged from turning to the past or to the future in times of anxiety. "One couldn't stay in the present moment. It was oppressing and frightening. [...] Some people went to seek the paradise of the old times, others followed the idea of a future paradise"[33] (transl. by E.M.B.).

3. Silence. The appreciation of silence generally characterizes northern people, who enjoy being close to nature. According to Pohjanen, silence in Meänmaa is associated with the ecstasy of a deeper existentialist understanding:

33. In the original: *"Nykyhetkheen ei saatu jää'ä. Se ahisti ja pölätti. [..] Toiset lähit hakheen paratiisiä entisistä aijoista, toiset lähit juovathaan tulevaisuuen paratiisin aatosta"* (Pohjanen 2011b, 74).

Eikös Meänmaan liikutukset ole hiljaisuuen vastakohta? Niin saattaa vaikuttaa ulkopuolisille, mutta mie olen huomanu, ette hiljasuuen filosofiin

päämäärä oon liikutus, kreikankielelä ekstasis. Liikuttunnu ihminen oon ulkonaisesti liikkuva, mutta sen sisin saattaa olla likelä tietämisen korkeinta astetta.
(Pohjanen 2011c, 78–79)

'Isn't the religious ecstasy of Meänmaa the opposite of silence? It might seem so to the outsiders, but I have observed that the main aim of the philosophy of silence is the emotional effect of ecstasy itself, called ekstasis in Greek. A person in an ecstatic state is moving as seen from the outside, but his/her deepest self might be close to the highest level of knowledge.'
(transl. by E.M.B.)

4. Ambivalent attitude towards the holders and representatives of political power. They are respected as long as they do not interfere with people's lives. However, loyalty towards the kings of Sweden has always been very strong: "The king is our guardian and the queen our wet nurse"[34] (transl. by E.M.B.).

5. Religious revival movements such as laestadianism and korpelanism also influenced the "canonization" of political personalities like Stalin or Lenin (Pohjanen 2011e, 83–84). According to Pohjanen, the inner need of people to venerate role models can easily lead to situations which might seem stunning to outsiders.[35]

6. Meänmaa has its own literature and it is written in Meänkieli. "Our own language and ethnicity is the basis of Meänmaa's literature. Its language is Meänkieli"[36] (transl. by E.M.B.).

7. The Meänmaa-philosophy is deconstructive in the sense that it dares to demolish the Swedish colonial discourse on Meänkieli language and culture. "Only literature in Swedish is accepted to describe also minorities. This is a well-known phenomenon for us in Meänmaa and Sapmi [= the land inhabited by the Sami]. Talking about this is still sensitive"[37] (transl. by E.M.B.).

8. Meänkieli-speaking people in Sweden identify themselves as Swedish. Minority status is not accepted nowadays unless it offers some material advantage.

34. In the original: *"Kuninkas oon meän holhooja ja trotninki meän imettäjä"* (Pohjanen 2011d, 81).

35. Similar situations can be observed for example in Csángó homes in Romania, where pictures of Jesus, as well as of political leaders can be found side by side on their home walls.

36. In the original: *"Kieli ja etnisiteetti oon Meänmaan kirjalisuuen perusta. Se oon meänkielinen"* (Pohjanen 2011f, 86).

37. In the original: *"Vain kirjalisuus, joka oon ruottalainen hyväksythään kuvvaahmaan minuriteettiäki. Tämä oon tuttu ilmiö meile Meänmaassa ja Sapmessa. Tästä puhuminen oon vieläki arka"* (Pohjanen 2011f, 86).

"Met olima ruottalaisia. Sitte tuli nuorempi polvi, joka ei ennää löysihamphaita tarvinu. Se teki politiikkaa asiasta, ko niilä ei muuta hommaa ollu, ja niin met saima kielelisen minuriteettiaseman ja sitä mukkaa vähän rahhaaki, mutta sillon havathiinki, ette perhana viekhöön, meitä meänkielisiä oon niin vähän, ettei meitä räkkää ees minuriteetiksi"
(Pohjanen 2011h, 92).

We were Swedish. Then a younger generation came and it did not need the false teeth[38] any longer. They politicized this issue, because they didn't have better things to do, and so we have got linguistic minority status and with it some money, too, but then it was realized that, damn it, we Meänkieli speakers are too few to even comprise a minority.
(transl. by E.M.B.)

38. The term used by Pohjanen symbolizes being second-class citizens because of the minority mother tongue.

9. Sauna is central to Meänmaa's culture. "The lecture-room of Meänmaa's philosophy is the sauna, with its roots in the age-old Finnish soil"[39] (transl. by E.M.B.).

10. *Sinni*, the Meänkieli equivalent of the Finnish *sisu*, meaning 'perseverence', 'persistance', 'tenaciousness' is one of the main characteristics of Meänkieli people. This quality also implies a dose of stubbornness.

All these characteristics generate some sort of mythical world, an imagined community of Meänmaa, which can be really understood by its in-group, or the members who share the same language and culture.

39. In the original: *"Meänmaan filosofiin opintosali oon sauna, sen juuret ikivanhassa suomalaisessa maaperässä"* (Pohjanen 2011i, 94).

7. Similarities and differences between Transylvanism and Meänmaa-idea

In comparing the two ideologies, I compare Transylvanism as cultural regionalism to Pohjanen's idea of Meänmaa.

Making virtue out of necessity was a common aim of the two ideologies; to replace the negatively charged minority status with positive options that are true to Transylvanian and and Meänmaa values. Beginning with the 1920s, the symbols of pearl and sand have become very common in Transylvanian Hungarian literature. It is the symbol of the "productive pain" caused to Hungarians by the Treaty of Trianon, a kind of moral answer to the historical and psychological shock they had experienced (Cs. Gyímesi 1992, 10). Thus, it is used as a moral symbol, involving a disharmony between a negative cause and a positive effect. In the literary works of Pohjanen, symbols, metaphors and comparisons abound which imply the ambivalence of shame and pride of the minority situation. However, pride is always dominant in him.

1. The main feature of both Transylvanism and Meänmaa-ideology has been the activism they promoted. Both ideologies emerged from the assessment of a historical situation which could not be changed. Kós declared that "Somewhere something was signed, somewhere something was negociated, somewhere something was divided; somewhere a door was slammed, so that it should remain closed for ever"[40] (transl. by E.M.B.). Pohjanen wrote about a very similar situation, referring to his own community:

> *Rajalinjaksi tuli väylänkurkku, jota oon sanottu kuninkhaan mustaksi nauhaksi. Tästä tuli Venäjän ja Ruottin raja. Se veethiin kysymättä kansalta ja huolimatta siitta, ette se halkasi suvut ja kultturellisen ykseyen.*
> (Meänmaa 2008)
>
> 'The deepest drift of the river became the frontier line, which was called the black band of the Tsaar. This became the border between Russia and Sweden. The border was drawn without asking for the people's permission and without taking into consideration the fact that it split families and a cultural unity.'
> (transl. by E.M.B.)

Both the Transylvanists and Pohjanen have striven to inspire the members of their communities to build a better future.

> *Fölébredtünk. Látni akarunk tisztán. Szembe akarunk nézni az Élettel, tisztában akarunk lenni helyzetünkkel. Ösmerni akarjuk magunkat. Számba kell vennünk erőinket, szerveznünk kell*

40. In the original: *"Valahol aláírtak valamit, valahol megalkudtak valamit, valahol elosztottak valamit; valahol egy ajtót becsaptak, hogy legyen az zárva örökre"* (Kós 1921, 1).

> *a munkát, tudnunk kell a célt, amit el akarunk érni.*
> (Kós 1921, 3)
>
> 'We have waken up. We want to see clearly. We want to face Life and be clear about our own situation. We want to know ourselves. We have to consider our forces, organize our work and we have to know the goal we want to achieve.'
> (transl. by E.M.B.)
>
> *Perustajitten aatos ja näky oon kaikkialla mailmassa elävien meänmaalaisten yhistäminen ja itenttiteetin vahvistaminen. Kieli oon sielun sormenjäljet. Met halvaama siksi tehhä työtä meänkielen hyväksi.*
> (Meänmaa 2008)
>
> 'The idea and the view of the founders was to unite all the Meänmaas who live all over the world and to strengthen their identity. Language is the fingerprint of the soul. That is why we aim to work for the benefit of Meänkieli.'
> (transl. by E.M.B.)

2. Both ideologies are based upon the idea that space can shape the spirit, and region is a particular outcome of its intercultural relations and diversity; although the culture of the minority's mother tongue must have a special place. Both Pohjanen and Kós emphasize the necessity of intercultural communication.

3. Transylvania and Meänmaa are, besides geographical and historical places, also cultural concepts. Meänmaa is a virtual space as well.

The Hungarians in Transylvania have loyalties to Romania, the state within which their home territory is situated and to Hungary, the state which their mother tongue and culture is part of. Having been part of the Hungarian nation, the Hungarian minority came under foreign rule. Nevertheless, their national culture and spiritual life persisted. They did not represent a regional variant of the Hungarian culture but were its heirs and developers in a new political situation. Thus, minority literature was able to create values which could really enrich the national culture.

This does not apply to the "citizens"[41] of Meänmaa, because their language is not spoken as the dominant language in a different state. Their loyalties lie with their homeland, Sweden, and with their regional culture.

4. Identification processes imply the construction of concrete and symbolic frontiers both in the case of Transylvanism and Meänmaa-ideology. Both minorities, Hungarians in Transylvania and Meänmaa people, discuss the separation of the in-group and out-group in their literatures. The main distinctive feature of the in-group is the minority language. Let me quote a clear passage from Pohjanen's autobiographical novel concerning the impossibility of mutual understanding between different language communities: *"Joila ruotti oon ensimäinen kieli asuva eri planeetoila ko met meänkieliset. Net ei meän asioita käsitä ollenkhaan"* 'Those whose first language is Swedish live on quite a different planet from us, the Meänkieli. They can't perceive our things at all' (Pohjanen 2014, 158).

5. Transylvanist writers and Pohjanen agree that minority literature has to be written in the minority language of the community. It is especially important when speaking of Meänkieli, a highly endangered language. The availability of literature written in the minority language can make the minority revise their belief, forced upon them by the majority, that their language is worthless.

The trauma of Romanian assimilation politics against Hungarians in Transylvania and the one of Swedish assimilation politics against Meänkieli-speaking Tornedalians are recurring themes in the literature of these two minorities.

6. The hierarchy of values is very similar in the two ideologies: birthplace – homeland – universal. Local values are believed to enrich values at the homeland level as well as those on the largest scale (universal). According to the two ideologies, minority literature is most closely linked to universal values through the topics it deals with. The "minority humanism" often mentioned by the Transylvanists is interpreted as protecting against nationalism. As Sándor Makkai presents it, the culture

41. It is interesting to notice that in Meänkieli there is no equivalent for the term 'citizen', only 'subject/vassal'. This mere fact tells a lot about the attitude Meänkieli people have had as to their status in Sweden.

of independent states (i.e. majority culture) inevitably obeys the prevailing political interests while the minority culture is free of them. Minorities are predestinated, through the suffering they are experiencing, to create a universal human spirituality (Makkai 1937).

7. Neither the Transylvanists nor Pohjanen elaborated on a well-defined or systematised ideology. Their ideologies can be most appropiately interpreted as a flexible ideas adjusted to the personal convictions of the people they represent.

8. Conclusions

In conclusion it is noteworthy that the two ideologies emerged in different geographical, historical, political and cultural circumstances. Transylvanism had a strong political charge while Meänmaa-ideology did not. Before the second half of the 19th century, the term Transylvanism was used in a cultural sense, meaning the uniqueness of Transylvanian cultural and political traditions. It became politically charged only after 1867 (when Transylvania and Hungary united). The emergence of interwar Transylvanism was the consequence of geopolitical changes after World War I. It happened as a reaction of Hungarian intellectuals to the fact that Transylvania was attached to Romania through the Treaty of Trianon. According to the intellectuals, Transylvanism meant autonomous Transylvania.

The emergence of Meänmaa-ideology was due to the work of a single man, Bengt Pohjanen, the revitalizer of Meänkieli language and culture almost two centuries after the political changes in Scandinavia leading to the splitting of the Finnish-speaking population in the Torne River Valley. However, encountering similarities between two minority ideologies born in different social, geographical, cultural and political contexts and in different times represents an interesting challenge for the researcher.

Let us return to the title of this study. During my research I came to the conclusion that inter-war Transylvanism is honoured on a much larger scale in Transylvania than Meänmaa-ideology has been in the Torne Valley. The main reason for this difference might lie in the two types of national identity, the Western European type, based on the concepts of country and citizenship, and Eastern European type, based on the concepts of ethnic origin and culture (Veres 2005, 88). It is interesting how exceptional Bengt Pohjanen is in the Swedish intellectual context and how incredibly close his concept of the essence of minority person is to Hungarian intellectuals' views in Transylvania. It is no wonder that while the voice of Károly Kós was "the voice of one calling in the wilderness" in the case of Bengt Pohjanen it has been a "voice crying in the wilderness".

Many people from Western cultures might consider both Transylvanist and Meänmaa-ideology provincial. In common thinking the proper word for the cult of local values is provincialism. Most of the minority cultures are wary of being called provincialist in a world striving to globalize. I myself as a researcher accept the view according to which province can enrich national and universal culture as well, and when Transylvanism and Meänmaa-ideology imply a kind of captiveness, at the same time it protects the community from being assimilated in a melting pot of universalism.

In a world of shifting identities and languages, as well as in the context of inter- and multicultural and multilingual exchange, the aim of this study is also to highlight the attempt of some minority language-speaking writers to make a contrast between their language and culture and the majority language and culture, as well as to create and/or reinforce the identity of their own ethnic and linguistic group.

List of references and sources

Andersson, Paula, and Raija Kangassalo. 2003. 'Suomi ja meänkieli Ruotsissa.' In *Monena suomi maailmalla*, edited by Hannele Jönsson-Korhola and Anna-Riitta Lindgren, 30–163. Helsinki.

Arola, Laura, Elina Kangas, and Minna Pelkonen. 2013. *Meänkieli Ruottissa. Raportin yhtheenveto ELDIA-projektissa.* Research Consortium ELDIA. Mainz.

Bible Hub. Accessed March 19, 2016. http://biblehub.com/john/1-23.htm.

Cs. Gyímesi, Éva. 1992. *Gyöngy és homok. Ideológiai értékjelképek az erdélyi magyar irodalomban.* Bukarest.

Gömöri, George. 2013. 'Introduction to Jenő Dsida's Poems. Poems translated by George Gömöri and Clive Wilmer.' *Hungarian Review* 4 (4). Budapest. Accessed March 16, 2016. http://www.hungarianreview.com/article/introduction_to_jeno_dsidas_poems_poems_translated_by_george_gomori_and_clive_wilmer.

Heikkinen, Vesa. 2012. 'Ideologia.' In *Genreanalyysi – tekstilajitutkimuksen käsikirja*, edited by Vesa Heikkinen, Eero Voutilainen, Petri Lauerma, Ulla Tiililä, and Mikko Lounela, 112–119. Helsinki. (=Kotimaisten kielten keskuksen julkaisuja, 169).

Holy Bible. New International version (NIV). 1973. Accessed March 16, 2016. https://www.biblegateway.com/quicksearch/?quicksearch=i+am+the+voice+of+one+calling&qs_version=NIV.

Institutul național de statistică. Recensământul populației şi al locuințelor. 2011. Accessed March 5, 2016. http://www.recensamantromania.ro/noutati/volumul-ii-populatia-stabila-rezidenta-structura-etnica-si-confesionala/.

K. Lengyel, Zsolt. 2007. *A kompromisszum keresése. Tanulmányok a 20. századi transzszilvanizmus korai történetéhez.* Csíkszereda. Accessed March 16, 2016. http://adatbank.transindex.ro/cedula.php?kod=734.

Kocsis, Károly, and Eszter Kocsis-Hodosi. 1998. *Ethnic Geography of the Hungarian Minorities in the Carpathian Basin.* Budapest.

Kós, Károly. 1921. 'Kiáltó szó Erdély, Bánság, Kőrösvidék és Máramaros magyarságához.' In *Kiáltó szó. A magyarság útja. A politikai aktivitás rendszere*, edited by Kós Károly, Zágoni István, and Paál Árpád. Kolozsvár. Accessed March 16, 2016. http://adatbank.transindex.ro/html/cim_pdf1374.pdf.

Láng, Gusztáv. 1998. *Kivándorló irodalom. Kísérletek.* Kolozsvár.

Makkai, Sándor. 1937. 'Nem lehet.' *Láthatár* 2: 49–53. Budapest. Accessed March 19, 2016. http://adatbank.transindex.ro/html/cim_pdf1527.pdf.

Meänmaa – rajaton kieli, kansa ja mieli. Accessed March 18, 2016. http://www.meanmaa.net/index_mmy.htm.
Nagy, Imola Katalin. 2014. 'Transylvanianism as Identity Discourse.' *Acta Universitatis Sapientiae, Philologica* 6 (3): 317–333. Cluj-Napoca.
Accessed March 19, 2016. http://www.diacronia.ro/ro/indexing/details/A16880/pdf.
Pohjanen, Bengt. 2011a. 'Meänmaas filosofi – finns den? Meänmaan filosofii – oonkos sitä?' In *Tungan mitt i munen. Kieli keskelä suuta*, edited by Bengt Pohjanen, 70–72. Luleå. (=Tornedalica, 61).
— 2011b. 'Meänmaas filosofi – hunger och dyrtid. Meänmaan filosofii – luppokauet.' In *Tungan mitt i munen. Kieli keskelä suuta*, edited by Bengt Pohjanen, 73–75. Luleå. (=Tornedalica, 61).
— 2011c. 'Meänmaas filosofi – en ripas skrift i snö. Meänmaan filosofii – riekon kirjotukset lumessa.' In *Tungan mitt i munen. Kieli keskelä suuta*, edited by Bengt Pohjanen, 77–79. Luleå. (=Tornedalica, 61).
— 2011d. 'Meänmaas filosofi – vår förmyndare och vår amma. Meänmaan filosofii – meän hohlooja ja imettäjä.' In *Tungan mitt i munen. Kieli keskelä suuta*, edited by Bengt Pohjanen, 79–82. Luleå. (=Tornedalica, 61).
— 2011e. 'Meänmaas filosofi – feber och hypokondri. Meänmaan filosofii – feeperi ja simylantit.' In *Tungan mitt i munen. Kieli keskelä suuta*, edited by Bengt Pohjanen, 82–85. Luleå. (=Tornedalica, 61).
— 2011f. 'Meänmaas filosofi – i Stockholm. Meänmaan filosofii oon jo Stockholmissa.' In *Tungan mitt i munen. Kieli keskelä suuta*, edited by Bengt Pohjanen, 85–88. Luleå. (=Tornedalica, 61).
— 2011g. 'Meänmaas filosofi – död hinner man ju alltid vara. Meänmaan filosofii – kuola met kuiten ossaama.' In *Tungan mitt i munen. Kieli keskelä suuta*, edited by Bengt Pohjanen, 88–91. Luleå. (=Tornedalica, 61).
— 2011h. 'Meänmaas filosofi – filosofiskt tal till minoriterna. Meänmaan filosofii – filosooffinen

puhe vähemistöile.' In *Tungan mitt i munen. Kieli keskelä suuta*, edited by Bengt Pohjanen, 91–94. Luleå. (=Tornedalica, 61).

– 2011i. 'Meänmaas filosofi – sauna. Meänmaan filosofii – sauna.' In *Tungan mitt i munen. Kieli keskelä suuta*, edited by Bengt Pohjanen, 94–97. Luleå. (=Tornedalica, 61).

– 2011j. 'Meänmaas filosofi – sinni. Meänmaan filosofii – sinni.' In *Tungan mitt i munen. Kieli keskelä suuta*, edited by Bengt Pohjanen, 97–100. Luleå. (=Tornedalica, 61).

– 2011k. 'Meänmaas filosofi – noetisk filosofi. Meänmaan filosofii – mielen filosofii.' In *Tungan mitt i munen. Kieli keskelä suuta*, edited by Bengt Pohjanen, 102–104. Luleå. (=Tornedalica, 61).

Pohjanen, Bengt. 2014. *The Smuggler King's Son.* Translated by Betty Léb. Manuscript.

Pomogáts, Béla. 1983. *A transzilvánizmus. Az Erdélyi Helikon ideológiája.* Budapest.

Sulkala, Helena. 2010. 'Introduction. Revitalization of the Finnic minority languages.' In *Planning a new standard language. Finnic minority languages meet the new millenium*, edited by Helena Sulkala, and Harri Mantila, 8–26. Helsinki. (=Studia Fennica Linguistica, 15).

Tánczos, Vilmos. 2000. 'Keletnek megnyilt kapuja.' In *Keletnek megnyilt kapuja*, edited by Tánczos Vilmos, 88–159. Csíkszereda.

Tolcsvai Nagy, Gábor. 2009. 'Ideologikus nyelvészeti sztereotípiák a magyar nyelvről.' In *Nyelvideológiák, attitűdök és sztereotípiák*, edited by Borbély Anna, Vančoné Kremmer Ildikó, and Hattyár Helga, 75–85. Budapest.

Török, Zsuzsanna. 2003. 'Transylvanism: A Politics of Wise Balance? Minority Regionalism in Interwar Romania. (1918–1940).' In *Regionale Bewegungen und Regionalismen in europäischen Zwischenräumen seit der Mitte des 19. Jahrhunderts*, edited by Philipp Ther, and Holm Sundhaussen, 127–144. Marburg. (=Tagungen zur Ostmitteleuropa-Forschung, 18). Accessed March 19, 2016. https://www.herder-institut.de/fileadmin/user_upload/pdf/

vergriffene_Publikationen/Herder_Institut_Tagungen_Band18.pdf.
Veres, Valér. 2005. 'Identitate etnică vs. Identitate națională în poziție minoritară. Cazul maghiarilor din Transilvania.' *Altera* 11 (26/27): 87–101. Tîrgu-Mureş.
Winsa, Birger. 2005. 'Language Planning in Sweden.' In *Language Planning and Policy in Europe,* Vol. 1, edited by Robert B. Kaplan, and Richard B. Baldauf Jr., 233–330. Hungary.

On the history of translation into Udmurt

Vera Grigorievna Panteleeva

1. Introduction

An electronic bibliographic index "Literary texts translated in Udmurt", containing 4152 units of bibliographic descriptions of translated fictional texts and individual works, was issued in Udmurtia in 2009. The electronic index reflects a huge amount of fiction and poetry translated into Udmurt since the first half of the 19th century. The index includes almost all literary texts translated into Udmurt.

This index is the "first page" in studying the history of translation into Udmurt. The priority tasks include the research of a number of problems, such as periodization of the history of translated literature. The two-century history of this process should be considered as a part of the historical and evolutionary process, with each certain stage having its own specifics, due to both the history of the Udmurt literature and language as well as the history of Russian (Soviet) literature. It is also important to take into consideration that the phenomenon of "translated literature", along with the translated texts of secular literature, also incorporates the translated texts of religious character, for the clerical component in the history of the development of any literature is essential in shaping its identity.

Considering all the factors, the history of translation into Udmurt can be roughly divided into five stages:

1. beginning of the 19th century – beginning of the 20th century
2. beginning of the 20th century – 1918
3. 1918 – the middle of the 20th century
4. middle of the 20th century – middle of the 1980s
5. middle of the 1980s – to present.

The boundaries of the designated stages are vague, mainly due to the lack of fundamental research on the issue.

2. Beginning of the 19th century – beginning of the 20th century

The chronological frame is determined by the phenomena connected with the formation of literacy and literature in Udmurt. Publication of the grammar of Udmurt (1775), which coincided with the process of the Christianization of the ethnic minorities of the Volga region and the Urals, gave a powerful impetus to the translation activity. The existence of "extensive translation practice in the beginning of the nineteenth century" (Shklyaev 2006, 332) is analyzed by A. N. Uvarov (Uvarov 1982, 5–51; Uvarov, 1994), A. G. Shklyaev (Shklyaev 2006, 329–339), B. I. Karakulov (Karakulov 1991, 115–123; Karakulov 2006), and V. K. Kelmakov (Kelmakov 2008). The monograph by Uvarov contains the most comprehensive list of the texts translated into Udmurt within the period of 1824 to 1917. Most of the texts are the translations of books and other texts of religious character, such as the Gospels, hagiographies, etc. To illustrate this period Shklyaev refers to the prayers translated into Udmurt and included into "Experiments of explaining the Christian beliefs." (Ilminsky 1885). Shklyaev argues that these texts have not yet been introduced into academic research (Shklyaev 2006, 332).

The other cornerstone of this period is the translation of the Gospels into Udmurt, made in 1904 by I. S. Mikheev. Analyzing the translation of the Gospels in that period, Uvarov comes to the conclusion that the texts of the Gospels translated into Udmurt before Mikheev (translations of 1847, 1880, 1882) are difficult to understand, because they are characterized by the abundance of Church Slavic words and the syntax is not typical of Udmurt (Uvarov 1994, 12). Meanwhile, the researcher greatly appreciated translation of the Gospels by Mikheev. According to Uvarov, Mikheev skillfully adapted the texts of the Gospels to the Udmurt reader by means of including colloquialisms and idioms. Mikheev was also the first among the translators into Udmurt to use the footnotes. Uvarov points out that "the development of modern Udmurt literary language originates from the translation of the Gospels by I. S. Mikheev" (Uvarov 1994, 13).

The first stage in the history of the Udmurt translated literature coincided with converting Udmurts to Christianity. Therefore, the first translation committees in the territories of Kazan and Vyatka provinces were established as clerical organizations that included the Bible Society Committee in Vyatka (1803), Kazan Orthodox Missionary Society (1864), Kazan Teacher Seminary for Non-Russian Population (1872). Among the first translators into Udmurt were local priests, teachers, merchants, and some of them did not have a good command of Udmurt. Therefore, discussing the aesthetic value of the first phase of translation into Udmurt might be premature.

The biggest role in the formation of translation into Udmurt belongs to G. E. Vereshchagin (1851 – 1930), the first Udmurt ethnographer, poet, and educator, as well as the first translator of artistic works into Udmurt ("The Tale of the Fisherman and the Fish" by A. S. Pushkin was translated by Vereshchagin in the 1880s) and the author of the first critical article on the problems of translation into Udmurt (Vereshchagin 1895). Today, there is extensive literature on his versatile creativity; the profound analysis of all the aspects of his activities is made by V. M. Vanyushev (Vanyushev 1995). For the initial phase of the history of the Udmurt literature G. E. Vereshchagin was the key figure. He was the first among the Udmurts to realize the importance of translations from other languages in order "to develop the national consciousness, or [...] to develop the education" (Chernyshevsky 1948, 503). Although his translation of the fairy-tale by Pushkin was not published during his lifetime, and its manuscript was discovered only in the 1960s, Vereshchagin's input into the development of translation into Udmurt is invaluable.

3. Beginning of the 20th century – 1918

Although the period under review covers approximately 15 years, it had a significant impact on the tradition of translation into Udmurt. These years were a turning point in the sense that there was a gradual shift of translation guidelines, according to which translation experiments were orientated at Russian revolutionary-democratic songs, fables, civic and pastoral poetry, didactic children's stories, and individual episodes of dramatic works (Ermakov 1981) which led to the formation of literature of a European type. The formation and development of secular culture was based on the translation of the works of Russian literature (fairy tales by A. Pushkin, poems by A. Koltsov, children's stories by L. Tolstoy and G. Ushinsky, etc.), although the process was largely spontaneous. Therefore, there were cases of translating the texts on the topic of the day, and the translation technique was often limited to word for word or literal translation.

One of the landmarks of that epoch was the translation of the poem by A. Pushkin "If life deceives you ...", made in 1918 by the first Udmurt poetess Ashalchi Oki (1898 – 1973). The translation is characterized by a number of peculiarities. Firstly, it is important that no one before Ashalchi Oki had ever translated into Udmurt a lyrical or philosophical poem that was devoid of any practical use and moralistic framework. For the Udmurt literature it was a new impulse, a new trend. Secondly, although this text was Ashalchi Oki's first and last experiment in translation, the Udmurt version of the poem is perfect in terms of the tonality of the text, its imagery and language. The translation is made at a high level and has not lost its poetic charm even today.

4. 1918 – the middle of the 20th century

The third period of the history of translation in the Udmurt literature is both interesting and controversial. A huge amount of factual material is contained in monographs by K. N. Dzuina (Dzuina 1976) and F. K. Ermakov (Ermakov 1981). According to Dzuina, in this period, which also includes the 1940s, when the translation and publication activities were practically nullified, a total of 395 texts were translated and published, i.e. nearly one hundred books a decade. Along with the classical heritage of the Russian literature, among the texts translated into Udmurt there were the texts of the contemporary authors. This trend was the part of the strategy aimed at the development and improvement of the quality of the Udmurt literature: for many authors of non-Russian literatures translation became the school of literary craftsmanship. This thesis, voiced in an article by the classic of the Udmurt literature M. Petrov (1905 – 1955), was perceived almost literally.

In the hierarchy of the Udmurt translators of this period the first place belongs to Kuzebay Gerd (1898 – 1937), one of the founders of the Udmurt literature, writer, poet, folklorist, ethnographer, and linguist, who translated from Russian into Udmurt and vice versa. His translation activities are partly analyzed by researchers (Kamitova 2006).

Kuzebay Gerd is the first professional translator of Udmurt literature. His literary education received at the Supreme Literary and Art Institute named after Brusov in Moscow (1922 – 1925) and rich bilingual translation experience prove it. He was a talented translator, with a keen sense for the choice of texts for translating: for example, he translated a large amount of literature for children, thereby filling a gap in the Udmurt children's literature. He also translated works of different genres (a fable, a triolet, etc.). He was the first to develop the professional strategy of literary translation among Udmurt translators: according to Gerd, translated works must be equal to the original in terms of artistic influence on the reader. These postulates can be illustrated by the translation experience of Gerd in 1919 – 1920 and 1924 – 1926: at this time on the pages of a proletarian newspaper "Gudyri" he published a number of translated works, including the revolutionary songs "Warszawianka", "La Marseillaise", "Boldly, comrades", as well as fables by I. Krylov and A. Cantemir. This period was marked by the debate in the press about the future of the national literary language: some authors called for the preservation of a single standard language, while others suggested the creation of two literary languages – North and South Udmurt. Gerd knew the progressive impact of translation in the process of regulation of a single literary standard language from first-hand experience and demonstrated the potentials of Udmurt in his own translating practice. In his translations he followed the methods of adequate, semantic translation and looked for specific linguistic techniques for "adaptation" of foreign language texts, e.g. using colloquialisms and idioms, well-known to the majority of readers. He widely practiced footnotes in which he explained the lexical meanings of words which could be new for his readers.

It is significant that even Udmurt literary critic A. S. Butolin in his pamphlet "Questions of terminology and translation in the Udmurt language" (1937), published after the persecution and execution of Gerd, in spite of accusing him of being "a bourgeois nationalist" (Butolin 1937, 36), recognizes his individuality and talent of a translator.

> Poetic imagery can be translated in three ways: 1. the exact translation of the vocabulary of phrases and structures enclosing the image; 2. restructuring phrases while maintaining the most important elements of the vocabulary; 3. substituting the original image by corresponding equivalents of the Udmurt language, closely in tune with the image of the original. The third way is the most daring and the most responsible reception. [...] The translation practice in the Udmurt language often deals with the first method. The second method is used rarely, and the third method is not used at all (with an exception of nationalist practices of Gerd in the translations of Krylov's fables and other nationalists translating Lermontov, Pushkin, etc. (Butolin 1937, 35–36)

Apparently, Gerd's talent was so great that it could not be hidden, but at the same time his work could not be appreciated directly, so his named was mentioned in the parentheses.

The strategy focused on the reader's perception of a literary work is characteristic for Gerd's translation from Russian into the Udmurt language, including the translation of his own poetry. The autotranslation practice of Gerd ("Wind of Uyshor", "Keremet", "We sow and sow ...") is to some extent beyond translation in the traditional sense, for, working in two languages, Gerd created two individual poems with similar motives, and the secondary (Russian) poetic text was often superior to the original. It was quite justified in the socio-cultural conditions of the functioning of the two literatures (Udmurt and Russian), when the artistic and aesthetic levels of the literatures were objectively different.

Unfortunately, many generations of Udmurt translators did not have access to Gerd's progressive literary heritage until 1960, and could not get rid of literalism which led to an abundance of Russianisms and coinages in the translated texts. Due to the fact that the progressive translation strategy of Kuzebai Gerd was not noticed in time, the qualitative development of translation activity in the Udmurt language was suspended for many years.

Udmurt children's literature of this period largely functioned in the form of translation texts rather than in the original. Selected publications included fairy-tales from the languages of the USSR, tales by European classical authors and compilers of folklore (Perrault, Andersen, the Brothers Grimm, etc.), short stories about Lenin, etc. As a result, from 1920s to the middle of the 20th century, a total of about 200 books for children and adolescents were translated and published into Udmurt, and many of them were reprinted. The number of copies of these books ranged from 5,000 to 15,000 books.

The third period in the history of translating into Udmurt is also interesting for the extension "of the literary geography" of translated works. The translators moved beyond Russian literature and began to explore different national cultures. For example, since the 1930s, there have been translations from the languages of the USSR and European languages. Thus in 1930s along with translations of the works by Ukrainian, Belarusian, and Latvian authors, there were translations of the texts by Hungarian, German, English, and French writers. None of the Udmurt translators of that time mastered the language of the original, therefore all the translations from other languages were made via Russian as the medium language.

It is also interesting that the translation into Udmurt is historically connected with the birth and the development of national press. Throughout the 20th century Udmurt newspapers and magazines more or less systematically and regularly published almost all translated literary works. Udmurt media, without even knowing it, created not only a kind of anthology of world literature translated, but in some way contributed to translating into Udmurt.

Translation activities of 1930s may also be referred to as the variety of "inner emigration" of the Udmurt writers who managed to survive during severe totalitarian regime and repressions. Avoiding any hot issue which could lead to prosecution, these few authors translated Russian classics and works by contemporary proletarian writers, e.g. poetry by N. Nekrasov, pastoral poetry by A. Pushkin and M. Lermontov, poems by V. Mayakovsky, prose and drama by M. Gorky.

The most prolific and fruitful translator of this period was M. Petrov. Judging by the number of translated works and individual books, no other translator could be compared with his input into the Udmurt literature. The peak of his legacy as a translator is marked by the translation of the poem "Vasily Terkin" by A. Tvardovsky, translated and published in 1952. This fact can be considered as the boundary, the final year of the third period which had a number of characteristics, such as the high level of translating skill, the maturity of the Udmurt literary language and new trends, and the Soviet translation studies after World War II. Post-war migration processes have generated unprecedented interest in the translation activities.

5. The middle of the 20th century – the middle of 1980s

In the peer-reviewed literature the 20th century has been called "the century of translation" (Toper 2000, 4).

> The beginning of the rapid development of the modern theory of translation is associated with the 1950s not by chance. The impetus for its development was a sharp change in the practice of translation that occurred in the middle of the last century and, accordingly, the public interest in this activity. One of the main reasons for these changes was the Second World War and political events, related to it directly or indirectly. (Garbovsky 2004, 171)

The period under review accounted for the decades when the idea of internationalism was fundamental in domestic and foreign policy of the USSR. With regard to the literatures of the peoples of the USSR, this idea sounded like a call for their "flourishing and convergence", that is why translating became the activity supported and controlled by the state. There is no doubt that the phenomenon of "multinational Soviet literature" could not function without literary translation.

In the history of the Udmurt literature this period is marked with paradoxical facts. On the one hand, the total number of translations of individual works of Soviet and foreign writers significantly increased, but, on the other hand, compared with the previous period the publication of translated books in the Udmurt language noticeably reduced. The translated literature was still mainly published in the newspapers, magazines and textbooks for primary school. The phenomenon can be explained by several reasons. Firstly, Russian-Udmurt bilingualism was becoming more and more common and, apparently, the Udmurt reader was orientated to read the Russian literature in the original. Secondly, translations often were of a casual character and were timed to the anniversary of this or another writer. Thirdly, in 1950 – 1970s the Udmurt literature still lacks texts for children, which is why translations from other languages were included into school textbooks.

In the Soviet republics of that period priority was given to the specific kind of bilingualism based on the combination of Russian and non-Russian language spoken in the region (Russian–Tatar, Russian–Chuvash, etc.). Udmurtia was no exception, that is why there were translations, for example, from Udmurt into Russian and vice versa, and unforgivably very few examples of translations in the area of Udmurt – other Finno-Ugric languages. Although in comparison with the previous decades the geography of translated works was larger and included other Finno-Ugric-literatures, interlanguage and inter-literature contacts could hardly be considered serious, due to the fact that the majority of the texts were the occasional works translated by occasional translators who do not speak the language of the original.

However, there was a pleasant exception:

> In 1975, in honor of the IV International Congress of Finno-Ugric Studies in Budapest a trilingual volume of poetry by Petofi (Udmurt-Russian-Hungarian) was published in a very beautiful design. The value of this small anthology lies in the fact that the translators (V. Kelmakov, G. Arkhipov) translated it from the original, because they know the Hungarian language. It was a nice gesture, but in general the Hungarian literature is represented in Udmurt very poorly, and often it does not refer to the true values or masterpieces [...].
> (Domokos 1993, 210–211)

The representation of the Udmurt literature in other Finno-Ugric languages was also irrelevant: during the Soviet period Finnish, Hungarian or Estonian translators did not demonstrate genuine interest towards the Udmurt literature. P. Domokos is absolutely right, claiming that,

> before admiring the signs of fraternal sympathy, we should understand that the mutual translations from one Finno-Ugric language to another were not made due to the familiarity with the literature and the language, but were based on the following: 1. Translation via Russian; 2. under the sign of the mandatory program of mutual acquaintance with the Soviet national culture; 3. and only in the last instance there was awareness that the translated text was originally written in a related language.
> (Domokos 1993, 221)

Meanwhile, the prevailing situation of isolation from closely related languages and literatures which occurred in Udmurtia is understandable, taking into account the objective and subjective reasons. The Republic as a whole, and Izhevsk in particular, was closed for any foreign visitors for almost the entire postwar period due to its military-industrial complex and the tension between the Soviet Union and the West. These factors were sure to have a negative impact on the national culture and literature development.

The analysis of the stylistic peculiarities of the translated texts of the period proves that the quality of translation significantly improved. The literal or word for word translation can be considered a thing of the past; the translators sought to capture and adequately convey the original features of the text being as well as to avoid many errors, e.g. the abundance of Russianisms. The losses that inevitably arise in the translation were compensated by individual stylistic techniques. Some of them succeeded to a greater extent (N. Bayteryakov, S. Perevoshchikov, V. Romanov, P. Pozdeev). These translators formed the basic strategy of poetic translation into Udmurt and raised the art of translation to a new level. Unfortunately, this positive experience is not properly researched and fully comprehended theoretically.

The final years of this period fall in the mid-1980s, which were characterized by political, social and economic changes in the country. The upheavals of this period radically altered the cultural and literary development in the national republics of Russia to the extent that we still have a number of problems rooted in these events. At the same time the changes in the society were generally favorable to the integration processes, including the field of translation.

6. The middle of the 1980s – to present

This period is an ongoing process, that is why it is hardly possible to have any generalizations, but emerging trends are noticeable. At first glance one can trace two oppositely directed vectors: on the one hand, there is a trend to enhance translation into Udmurt (Russian, Finno-Ugric and European literatures are perceived and interpreted by the Udmurt literature anew); on the other hand, there is a pursuit of the Udmurt authors to tell the world about themselves, i.e. there is activation of translation from Udmurt into the European and Finno-Ugric languages. In either case, there are pragmatic aspirations of the modern humanitarian sphere: in the 21st century literary translation goes beyond literature and entwines with the functions of PR-technologies as well as presents the conscious demonstration of one's ethnic identity in the context of globalization. In other words, translation is now involved in positioning and promotion of ethnic culture in the modern realities and becomes an integral part of popular cultural projects with a focus on ethnicity. Here are a few representative examples.

A new star has shone recently to present the Udmurt culture at an all-Russian and international level. *Buranovskiye babushki* ('Grannies from Buranovo') is a musical folklore ensemble from an Udmurt village of Buranovo. The team won the Russian Eurovision Contest of 2012 and was among the winners of the International Eurovision 2012 in Baku. The history of the project is connected with a concert in 2008 when the members of the ensemble, elderly Udmurt women, sang songs by Russian rock-singers Viktor Tsoi and Boris Grebenshchikov translated into Udmurt. The musical experiment aimed at a public shock achieved the goals of the authors of the project; today the repertoire *Buranovskiye babushki* is based on pop songs translated from Russian into Udmurt. Unfortunately, the translated variants of the lyrics are perceived by the public and critics as a secondary phenomenon, hardly anyone is interested in the personality of the translator, as the exotic settings and scenic images are considered to have a greater value.

In the 2000s the project "Russian classics in the Udmurt" was conceived in the same vein. Within the project poems by S. Esenin (2002), N. Nekrasov (2003), M. Lermontov (2005), A. Pushkin (2007), A. Koltsov (2009) and the full version of "Eugene Onegin" by A. Pushkin (2009) were published in individual volumes. Most of the works of the aforementioned authors (for example, their love poetry) had never been translated into Udmurt, therefore the translations demonstrated the modern translators' mastery and unlimited potentials of modern

Udmurt. This project is of great value to the Udmurt philology (comparative stylistics, the history of literary language) and bilingual education, but, unfortunately, it was implemented too late and failed to find its readers. Today many Udmurts are indifferent even to the Udmurt literature originally written in Udmurt, therefore, they will ignore these translations, preferring to read Pushkin in the original.

In general, in the period under review, the number of translations from Russian decreased in comparison with the translations from other Finno-Ugric languages. In the post-Soviet reality, collaboration between the Uralic literatures began to develop under new geopolitical conditions aimed at the formation of a multicultural space. Translation became one of the real mechanisms of the modern Finno-Ugric world for implementing integration policies in culture. The leaders of the Finno-Ugric ethnic and cultural movements are well-aware of this phenomenon. For example, the Estonian writer and culture expert Arvo Valton claims that

> the idea of the Finno-Ugric community without translation is just impossible. At a time when the native languages of our eastern cousins are prevalent mostly in kitchens, we, the islands that once used to unite the whole continent, have to stick together. Translation is the bridge that allows you to get from one island to another and communicate with each other.
> (Devitsyn 2010)

The first interesting experiments of translating from other Finno-Ugric languages occurred in the 1990s, especially within the Udmurt-Hungarian contacts. In 1997 the anthology of the Hungarian literature "Waves of the Danube – on the banks of the Kama River" was published in Udmurt for the first time. The collection of the masterpieces of the Hungarian literature translated into Udmurt was prepared in a book with a symbolic title by an Udmurt writer Vyacheslav Ar-Sergi and a Hungarian scholar, professor of the University of Szeged Istvan Kozmach, who mastered Udmurt at the level of proficiency.

Another positive moment is connected with the fact the new generation of Udmurt translators has a good command of Hungarian. They have all the opportunities to obtain professional skills in translating at the Udmurt Philology Faculty of the Udmurt State University as well as during their internships at the universities of Hungary. Thus, for example, the young Udmurt translators published the book of poetry by Jozsef Attila (2009) in Udmurt. Other new translations from Hungarian are regularly published in the local periodicals.

The Hungarian colleagues responded with a noble gesture. In 2004, in Budapest, they published the poetry of the Udmurt literature classics Ashalchi Oka and Kuzebai Gerd in bilingual (Hungarian-Udmurt) collections. Both books were compiled and edited by P. Domokos, who is also the author of a concise but deep preface. The poetic texts are translated by famous translator Anna Bede with the assistance of specialists from Udmurtia.

There is also mutual interest towards Udmurt-Finnish (and vice versa) translations. In 1995, a bilingual anthology of Udmurt poetry *"Suuren Guslin Kaiku"* ('The Song of Great Gusli') was published in Helsinki. It included 61 Udmurt poems by six poets representing different generations and different philosophies of poetry (K. Gerd, A. Oki, F. Vasiliev, A. Kuznetsova, L. Kutyanova, V. Vladykin), which recreated the most complete picture of the Udmurt poetry of the 20th century. The collection is also notable for the fact that, along with the translations made by the professor of the University of Helsinki Raya Bartens (who also speaks Udmurt), it contains original poetic texts, which greatly multiplies the value of the publication.

In 2010 an anthology of contemporary Russian Finno-Ugric literatures entitled "Volga" was published in Helsinki. The Udmurt literature was represented there by works of five authors, all the texts were translated from the original language, because the translator Esa-Jussi Salminen fluently speaks Udmurt.

The beginning of the new millennium was marked by the publication of the Finnish-Karelian epic *Kalevala* in a separate volume. The translator A. Uvarov worked on it for nearly three decades. Its first magazine version was published in 1985 and, although the translation generally received good reviews, the translator felt dissatisfied with the literal re-creation of the formal features of the original, e.g. the preservation of the feminine rhymes uncharacteristic of the Udmurt poetry. After long consultations with his colleagues – both scholars and translators – A. Uvarov came to the best option: octosyllabic verses of the Udmurt *Kalevala* have a combination of anapaest – iambus – anapaest and traditional Udmurt poetry rhyme. The Udmurt *Kalevala* belongs to the short translations of the epic, the Udmurt text has 8,500 verses while the original contains 22,795 verses.

Over the past ten years dozens of books have been translated into Udmurt from Estonian, which has become a precedent, for none of the Estonian authors had been represented in Udmutia by the publication of a separate book. Translation activities between the Udmurt and Estonian literatures became successful due to the creative tandem of Arvo Valton and Nadezhda Pchelovodova. As true *kulturträgers*, they are engaged in the promotion of the Estonian literature to the Udmurt readership, and the Udmurt literature – to the European reader.

Cooperation and partnership involve the talk “on equal terms”, and today it is recognized in the professional environment engaged with translation activities. Our experience demonstrates that there is a tendency to increase requirements to the quality of the original texts selected for translation as well as to the standards of translation itself. New generations of Udmurt translators who master Hungarian, Finnish, Estonian, German, English and other languages translate from the language of the original.

The two centuries of the history of translation in the Udmurt literature are heterogeneous in nature. The history of translation must be properly researched with a focus on its internal and external properties, including the stages of its periodization. The translated texts must be involved into the literary process to become the centerpiece of further analysis.

List of references and sources

Butolin, Andrey. 1937. *Questions of terminology and translation in the Udmurt language.* Izhevsk.

Chernyshevsky, Nikolay. 1948. *The Complete Works: The 15th vol.* Moscow.

Devitsyn, Vladimir. 2010. 'On the wings of the translation.' *Rossiyskaya Gazeta*, September 30.

Domokos, Peter. 1993. *Formation of the literatures of ethnic minorities of the Urals.* Yoshkar-Ola.

Dzuina, Klavdia. 1976. *Udmurt book of 1917 – 1974.* Izhevsk.

Ermakov, Foma. 1981. *Creative Communications Udmurt literature.* Izhevsk.

Garbovsky, Nicholay. 2004. *Theory of Translation.* Moscow.

Ilminsky, Nicholay.1885. *Experiments of explaining the Christian beliefs.* Kazan.

Kamitova, Alevtina. 2006. *Imaginative world of Kuzebai Gerd: the original translation and interpretation.* Izhevsk.

Karakulov, Boris. 1991. 'On the history of the written records of the Mari and Udmurt language.' In *Pre-revolutionary origins of interliterature community of the Ural-Volga region,* edited by Vasily Mikhailovich Vanushev, 115–123. Izhevsk.

– 2006. *The history of written Udmurt. XVIII – XXI centuries.* Izhevsk.

Kelmakov, Valey. 2008. *Essays on the History of the Udmurt language.* Izhevsk.

Perevoshchikov, Peter. 1937. 'How to translate Russian text on the Udmurt language.' *Journal of UdNII* 7: 43–51.

– 1940. *To improve the translation script.* Izhevsk.

– 1949. 'On measures to improve translation work.' *Journal of UdNII* 11: 64–83.

Shklyaev, Alexander. 2006. 'Critical thinking and the stages of formation of the Udmurt literary language.' In *Problems and prospects for the functioning of native languages,* edited by Z. Suvorova, 329–339.

Toper, Peter. 2000. *Translation in Comparative Literature System.* Moscow.

Uvarov, Anatoly. 1982. 'On the question of the formation of literature genres Udmurt pre-October period.' In *On the origins of the Udmurt literature,* edited by Zoia Alekseevna Bogomolova, Vasily Mikhailovich Vanushev, Tatiana Perevozchikova, 5–51.

– 1994. *Enlighteners*. Izhevsk.

Vanyushev, Vassiliy. 1995. *The artistic heritage of G.E. Vereshchagin in the context of national literatures of the Ural-Volga region*. Izhevsk.

Vereshchagin, Grigoriy. 1895. *About books on in the Votyak language*. Vyatka.

The Allegorisation of Minority Space in Slovakian Hungarian Literature

Anikó Polgár

1. Introduction[42]

Minority space is a medium that, in some respect, can be forced between boundaries and which can mean both an intimate, safe haven in the face of some (sometimes frightening) wideness or majority, and at the same time also a clutching discomfort and oppressing confinement. The space, which is in close connection with one's identity, shading or defining it, can be real or constructed. It can equally be associated with the alienating categories of isolation, externality, and an insiderness difficult to access from outside as well as with the positive concepts of belonging together, the common tradition reinforcing one's self-image and the adaptability aligned with it and also those of multiculturalism.

The close connection between space and identity is strongly reflected in literary representations. In the space of minority literature, too, the forms of interculturality are influenced by local characteristics,

42. This research was supported by grant VEGA 1/0051/14 Ideologies, identities and self-representation in the context of linguistics and literary theory within multicultural space.

social and political circumstances, since, as Johanna Domokos emphasizes:

> There are quite different challenges to face whether, for example, the literary field conquers a territory which had had relatively independent traditions (e.g. the relationship between the literary field in Finland and Swedish literature in Finland) or the majority blocks the development of minority literatures in the first place (e.g. the development of Sami literature in the Scandinavian literary field).
> (Domokos 2013, 42)

In my paper, I attempt to grasp the relationship between space and identity in the context of Hungarian literature in Slovakia. In the next sub-chapter, I will examine the interpretability of the concept of Hungarian literature in Slovakia, based on the concept of multiculturalism and minority literature. A separate sub-chapter deals with the issues of space and identity in the Hungarian literature in Slovakia, which places this topic in a wider context, approaching the meeting point of cultures from the perspective of hybridity. A further sub-chapter will show how the tales written by a Slovakian Hungarian female writer, Anikó N. Tóth, can be interpreted on the basis of cross-writing as allegorical stories including the multiculturalism of minority space and its attitudes to diversity.

2. The dilemmas of Hungarian literature in Slovakia

Before launching into our literary interpretations, it seems essential to clear up a conceptual confusion. It is the definition of one of our basic concepts: the term "Hungarian literature in Slovakia". It is so problematic that some scholars suggest abandoning it altogether (cf. Grendel 1998, 96–104; Németh 2005, 5–23). It is remarkable that the literary-historical use of the concept is not in accordance with attempts to grasp this space from a political, historical or linguistic aspect.

With reference to the indivisibility of the Hungarian literary space and the cohesive power of the language, literary historians emphasize that the Hungarian literatures over the national borders are linked to the mother country. They describe the necessary appearance of intersection points rather as a constraint or a pressure from the apparatus of power and regard it as the hotbed of provincialism, the way out of which should be a move towards universality. Consequently, the examination of the fertilizing effect of this multilingual and multicultural medium also becomes incidental. It is a fact that the presence or absence of features characteristic of the specific medium or those emphasizing multiculturalism cannot be regarded as an aesthetic category, but neither can the adherence to the trends of the mother country (which often escapes the attention of critics). Both the mother country's and the minority literary-historical discourse undeniably have their own anomalies, too. Emphasising the indivisibility of Hungarian literature is mainly in the interest of those stuck outside the mainstream, those wanting into the centre from the periphery, and is not necessarily in harmony with the wishes of those in the centre.[43]

43. Gergely Vida points out the one-sidedness of this view in connection with the scanty reception in Hungary of Hungarian poetic works created in Slovakia (Vida 2003, 173–177).

For example, if we compare the status of Hungarian literature in Slovakia to that of Swedish literature in Finland, (this parallel being supported by the common history of the minority and majority nations and the existence of a mother country), the differences in the communication of the majority and the minority are apparent. Whereas Finns definitely consider Swedish literature in Finland to be part of their own literature, in Slovak-Hungarian relations, the attempts made at the same were met with resistance because they reminded the minority writers of the methods of the colonists engulfing and draining the sap from their subordinates (cf. Polgár 2011, 149–157). Another reason that the correlation cannot work according to the Finnish pattern is that the vast majority of Slovak writers and literary historians do not read Hungarian. What is more, the channels directing Hungarian literature towards the Slovaks are diminishing and the new generations of Slovakian Hungarian authors do not turn to Slovak literature for inspiration (perhaps due to the aggressive methods of teaching the Slovak language in schools).

Nevertheless, the suggestion to reject the category "Slovakian Hungarian literature" was not derived from an objective literary-historical observation, but from a subjective, emotional basis: in its background, there is the rejection of literary collectivism, oppressive provincialism, and the forced role of being a bridge. In my opinion, however, this subjectivism, though reasonable from the writer's point of view, cannot be identical with that of the literary historian, whose job it is to also record the facts and interpret literary phenomena. It is expedient to broaden the categories "minority" and "majority", in the same sense as József Imre Balázs does in applying Deleuze-Guattari's concept of minority to Transylvanian Hungarian literature. He says:

> If we want to remain consistent in a train of thought that interprets Transylvanian Hungarian literature as »minority« (which is by no means the only possible approach, but let us keep it for the purposes of this paper), we must place the manner of speech of Transylvanian Hungarian literature in the context of not only one majority language and identity, as we usually think about it in terms of citizenship and politics, but in relation to all majority languages and identities.
> (Balázs 2006)

The question of the minority writer's choice of language cannot be narrowed down to the correlation of mother tongue–state language, as believed by Zoltán Németh, criticising the concept of Deleuze and Guattari (Németh 2013, 17). Quite the contrary: the writer's choice and creation of language is derived from the polyphony of countless language variants, as is well illustrated by the example of Kafka, writing in the German language of Prague and creating a unique literary form of expression on its basis. According to Deleuze and Guattari, Kafka had to find "his own point of underdevelopment, his own patois, his own third world, his own desert" (Deleuze and Guattari 1986, 18). Even though we are not talking about a literature written in the language of the majority like in the case of Kafka, but about the literature of a minority language, the other two characteristics of minor literature: political charge and the presupposition of collective values are also characteristic of the Slovakian Hungarian literary tradition. At the same time, in this case, linguistic "deterritorialization" can be grasped in the relationship of the minority to the mother country. From now on, I am using the term "minority literature" (as a synonym of "minor literature") on the basis of this concept and are going to find spaces which are, in some works of contemporary Slovakian Hungarian literature, minority not only in the geographical sense but also function as minor linguistic territories or, following the above metaphor, as one's own desert.

3. The possibilities of the interpretation of space

The characteristics of space become particularly striking when we are faced with the differences through moving from one medium to the next, that is, by travelling, wandering or migration (cf. Chambers 1994). However, from the aspect of space interpretation, the moving of country borders creates a unique situation, when individuals or communities, though not moving, find themselves within new circumstances. In one of his essays, Lajos Grendel ironically shows the forced movements of identity of those who stay in the same place, through the life story of a family in Košice (Grendel 1998, 12). During their long lives, the members of the Schmidt family, who never left their home town, were Hungarian and Czechoslovak citizens twice each, and finally they passed away as Slovak citizens.[44] Although it was not through immigration that Slovakian Hungarians found themselves in an intercultural medium (indeed, they did not have to move an inch to get across one or even more borders), the haphazard nature of immigrants also characterizes the state of being of the Slovakian Hungarian community, and this haphazardness can also be traced in literature. According to Iain Chambers, migration "calls for a dwelling in language, in histories, in identities that are constantly subject to mutation" (Chambers 1994, 5). Hungarians in Slovakia are between two states of being: inside and outside at the same time, "at the intersections of histories and memories" (Chambers 1994, 6). In this case, too, total identity is an imaginary construction, even if we are not aware of its uncertainties.[45]

44. Comparing the minority circumstances in Slovakia and Finland, Zuzana Drábeková draws attention to the Finns' similar experiences regarding Karelia (Drábeková 2014, 217).

45. Cf. Chambers 1994, 25: „[..] we are now beginning to learn to act in the subjunctive mode, 'as if we had' a full identity, while recognising that such a fullness is a fiction, an inevitable failure".

Recent definitions, which place minority literatures in space and grasp them in relation to space, usually include the ambivalences of identity as well. If we look at the theoretical definitions relating to German minority literature (*deutsche: Minderheitsliteratur*) in a monograph (Kirjuchina 2000) written about the poetry of a German minority in the Soviet Union (*Sowjetdeutsche Lyrik*), the movement towards issues of identity in the special literature becomes apparent. According to a definition from 1976, cited by the author, German minority literature is a literature born in the German language in a space determined by another, majority language (Kirjuchina 2000, 31). Another paper, written in 1982, interprets the literature of Germans living abroad as provincial literature and regards it as small art of regional orientation. German minority literature represents itself as a microcosm and models a world in opposition with the surrounding world (Kirjuchina 2000, 34). On the other hand, a monograph published in 2000 focuses on the issue of identity. Its basic hypothesis is that the literature of the German minority in the former Soviet Union can be interpreted as a narrative act of identity (Kirjuchina 2000, 9).

This experience can also bear fruit in the study of Hungarian literatures across the borders, as their status is similar: Hungarian literature born in a space determined by another, majority language. For a long time in Slovakian Hungarian literature, the provincial nature of this artificially created microcosm was emphasised. For a long time, it attempted to fashion itself according to expectations, but its latest expressions are often balancing between collective and individual identity, placing their identity issues in a wider context. In my opinion, it is not necessary to strictly differentiate (as done by Németh 2013, 23) between works that directly reflect on the Hungarian medium in Slovakia and those that deal with a more universal subject matter (e.g. works related to Ancient Greek or Latin myths) because, in an allegorical sense, the latter can also refer to the problems of identity originating from the dwindling of the minority space or the superimposition of different elements.

In her book, Holly E. Martin examines the meeting points of two or more cultures, among other things, highlighting that the representation of opposing places as symbols of cultural conflicts results in a hybrid perspective in literature (Martin 2011, 13). We can employ similar viewpoints in the interpretation of contemporary Slovakian Hungarian literature. For example, the main characteristic of Pál Száz's short prose (Száz 2017) is hybridity in language, genre, and style alike. The short prose texts created by the author, which belong to a unique genre (phyto-legends, phyto-anecdotes, phyto-aphorisms), are transformations of history. Not only do they retell and re-cite history but also re-situate historical and cultural knowledge. This transformation is most spectacular not on the level of stories or narratives but on that of the mode of narration. In the background of history, re-interpreted according to the private viewpoints of a small community, there is a harvested, collectible *corpus*. Its construction and composition, (which, for the time being, can only be traced in micro-structures, in magazine publications), serves to transform or at least re-colour this given.

The linguistic applications of hybridity are assisted by utterances from different sources. The writer uses the old Hungarian written tradition (the language and motifs of mediaeval legends), the written elements of the originally oral tradition of tales, which are regarded as the products of folk religion, as well as the direct oral tradition, which presents the memory of the small community and family memory screened through the current horizon of today. Pál Száz's short prose also provides us with the spaces of identity constructs. The plants filled with mystic meaning grow in a lyrically fictionalized historical space, whose most striking characteristic is multiculturalism, the presence of Hungarian, Slovak, Jewish, Turkish and Gypsy elements. This mystified space becomes, at the same time, the medium of a community in South Slovakia as well as that of a sacred literary manifestation, sublime and parodistic at the same time, which also demonstrates this hybridity in its language.

4. Spaces of hiding and wandering in the tales of Anikó N. Tóth

The tales of Anikó N. Tóth present the identifying role of space combined with the characteristics of a local dialect.

They are linguistically slightly less radical than Pál Száz's works and they use the elements of the Palots dialect, prevalent along the banks of the River Ipel', only for colouring material. The texts in the first two storybooks by Anikó N. Tóth, who lives in Šahy[46], can be read on two different levels in the spirit of cross-writing[47]: both as children's stories and also as allegories for adult readers.

46. Šahy is a small town in Southern Slovakia, near the border with Hungary.

47. This term was introduced into the research on children's literature by American U. C. Knoepflmacher. On the possible uses of the concept, see Kümmerling 2003, 277-296.

The opening text of the volume *Tamarind* is *The Smoke Carver's Tale* (N. Tóth 1994, 5–10), whose main character is Boldizsár, a smoke carving artisan, who is also a doctor and, on an eschatological level, the benefactor of humankind and the world. The smoke carver regards his job of cleaning chimneys as creative artwork. This story is a variation on the classic pattern of the magic tale, which ends with the wedding of the smoke carver, who saves the empire, and the youngest princess. It is embedded in a meta-poetic framework: the cloud of smoke hiding the magical world of tales and the all-enveloping soot constitutes the writer's own world. In the end Boldizsár, who carves stories out of the smoke, makes everyone like himself.

> Even the princess had learnt the art of smoke carving and, in order not to be different from her fellow-countrymen and especially from Boldizsár, she covered herself in a thick cloud of smoke to be black again. She has been carving the prettiest smoke flowers in the world ever since.
> (N. Tóth 1994, 10)

The Smoke Carver's Tale, like most Hungarian folk tales, ends in a state of completeness: a wedding and starting a family (cf. Boldizsár 2012, 232).

As it is a story that can also be interpreted allegorically, the author can naturally feel free to play with the pattern and typical motifs of magical tales. However, critics of the book were bothered by such deviations, for example, having four princesses instead of the usual three. "Ignoring the magic numbers of tales, there are four princesses", says Zsuzsanna Kozsár states disapprovingly (Kozsár 2002, 42). László Koczur shares her opinion: "And what comes then is really confusing: why does the king have four daughters? What is more, the increased number of princesses is completely useless and unfunctional in terms of the outcome" (Koczur 2003, 99). In my opinion, these attacks are rather misguided, as they disregard the fact that the number four is used in the tales for volume compositional considerations. That is, in *Tamarind*, there are several short writings called by the author '*fablettes*', arranged in groups of seven and the groups divided by four magic tales, equalling the number of the princesses (*A halványkék kisoroszlán* 'The Pale Blue Lion Cub', *Kaimómese* 'Kaimo Tale', and *Tamarind*, besides *The Smoke Carver's Tale*).

The opening tale carries allegorical meanings not only through such opposites as the artistic and the ordinary, the clean and the soiled, the above and the below, but also in terms of the depiction of spaces and the presentation of diversity. The smoke carver is separated from those around him by his unwashable blackness (cf. N. Tóth 1994, 5: "he was always smoky, despite washing himself often in the crystal-clear creek"). He is like an immigrant doing menial work or a Gypsy, who is different from the others in both complexion and way of life, doing service to all the citizens yet despised by all of them regardless of their social status. The text emphasises that he cleans the chimneys for all and sundry, from the dwellers of shanties and cottages to those of mansions and chateaux. Contempt against him does not cease even after the king appoints him master of chimneys. The princesses are curious about this weird newcomer yet, except for the youngest one, they do not talk to him nor accept his present. The fourth princess who, instead of stooping down to Boldizsár, must climb up to him onto the palace roof, even though curious, is first frightened by the blackness of Boldizsár's world: "She was so terrified of the cloud of smoke gushing out that she got dizzy and fell into the chimney" (N. Tóth 1994, 8). After the princess fell into the chimney and became unwashably black, her family does not recognise her and she is forced to hide and adopt Boldizsár's lifestyle. The community will duly be punished for segregating some of its members: the fourth princess is cleansed by some magic soap, but the unwashable soot settles upon the inhabitants of the palace and the city. The motif of wandering emerges during the search for the magic soap. Movement also entails the loss or at least the weakening of one's identity: "Boldizsár had wandered so long that he even forgot his name" (N. Tóth 1994, 9).

The tale novel entitled *Alacindruska* consists of short story-like episodes. In every episode, the reader is introduced to new characters, who often cross the boundaries between two worlds. The basic plot is actually nothing else but movement and wandering: a unique, story-like migration, the aim of which is to adapt to the one's new surroundings, and the obstacles arise from meeting strangers on one hand and from the hostile emotions of the locals (or natives, if you like) on the other. Kunka, the evil elf, who throws obstacles in the newcomers' way, feels cosy in his own space until a higher power, the Eagle, who binds up the beaks of songbirds and silences all song, puts him in the group of the small, weak and subordinate. The first tale starts with the wandering of Törpincs, and can be read as a story of mass migration. Törpincs, who can smell the fine fragrance of Alacindruska (the hyacinth flower), meets a bunch of dissatisfied creatures on his way, whom he persuades to join him. Their aim is not only to approach the fine fragrance but also to solve their psychological or existential problems: "We are looking for good spirits for Durmancs, decent clothes for Pacuka, friends for you, and in the meantime we'll find out where this fine fragrance comes from" (N. Tóth 1999, 6). Kunka, the naughty elf, manages to make the lives of those living around Alacindruska miserable.

The fate of the protagonists of another story, two fairies, Cinórka and Macúrka, is even more similar to the fate of immigrants than Törpincs'. Their previous dwelling place, the meadow, was mowed, so they are forced to leave their home and wander in the forest, startled by every new thing they see. "They stared in amazement, as they had never seen trees before" (N. Tóth 1999, 23). The fairies' occupation was to dust the flowers. One of them is encaged by Kunka, but Törpincs eventually help them to adapt to their new surroundings. "We are looking for a job, as our previous workplace is no more ..." – they complain after escaping the clutches of Kunka (N. Tóth 1999, 30).

Butyika, the hero of the tale entitled *Deaf Marsh*, is also looking for a new home. He cannot bear living in the reeds anymore because his neighbours, the mallards, are hassling him. However, he is captured in the deaf Marsh. When he starts whistling in the gloomy silence, the Eagle, who had recently moved to the marsh, catches him. The Eagle does not care for music, and he had bound up the beaks of songbirds and gathered all the birds in a pit. At last, they manage to escape with the help of Kunka, who had also fallen captive.

The place name *Palotsia* in the subtitle of the book designates a space created by the author for the tale's sake. Its boundaries are set by the language they use there. The words selected from the dialectal dictionary of the Palots region along the banks of the River Ipel', whose meaning is explained in an index annexed to the tales, are placed next to the strange-sounding names of herbs such as henbane, chervil, cammock, the presence of which helps the reader to both realistically position and mystify the space at the same time.

The allegorical interpretation becomes politically charged according to the situation at the time when the book was written. Both storybooks that I am analysing were published in the 1990s, after the change of political systems and the formation of independent Slovakia (1993) and they reflect the political changes in the attitudes towards minorities. The motifs of wandering and travelling also reflect the opportunities provided by the opening up of the borders after the political changes. The initial times of independent Slovakia (during the government of Vladimír Mečiar) was characterised by intolerance towards minorities, which can be felt in the tales through the elements of aggression against diversity and the attempt to silence other languages and voices. Besides silencing a mass of songbirds and bounding their beaks, a similar act is the forceful confiscation of Didirka's overcoat, which he had inherited from his great-grandfather. "I thought the forest was everybody's" – answers Didirka to his attacker, who answers from the point of view of the majority violently oppressing the minority: "Yes, of course, – snapped Gugonya. – But you're an exception!" (N. Tóth 1999, 43). The further course of the tale suggests that intolerance against the minority negatively impacts the majority, too: after confiscating the coat, not only its former owner but all the inhabitants of the forest are cold.

On an ethical level, the tales meet the usual expectations. They set oppositions, which are then resolved by traditional and contemporary fairytale turns. For example, Kandika's and Dülle's evil inclinations are driven out by sucking on bitter sweets. The forest creatures are finally united by the common enemy in an emergency situation. The refugees are fleeing from the unknown attackers who cut down the trees in the forest, thus endangering their habitat. They are running so fast that they can only carry their most essential belongings. What they most regret to leave is the countryside, their natural surroundings: the rocks, the grass, the branches. The creatures of the tale are hiding in a cave, longing for their lost homeland and also mourning the impossibility of return and the irreversibility of the past. After they manage to drive out the attackers with the magic word they received from Alacindruska, not only is order restored but even the former anomalies are put right: all the characters are feasting on the *pel'menis* that Mányi had made.

Palotsia turns into an idyllic countryside like Moominvalley, which is interpreted as the Swedish minority in Finland, and which is sometimes threatened by external dangers just like Palotsia (Drábeková 2011, 38). The tightness of the minority space is symbolised by the scenes in the tales which allow little movement or are completely closed, like the cage where Macúrka is kept prisoner; the rock cave, where the Eagle locked up the songbirds with bound-up beaks; the cave of the Chingo-rock, where the inhabitants of Palotsia hid from the wavals and the antangels (which are words to playfully scare children in the Palots dialect); and also the narrow piece of the moon which Pajod held grabbed after his ladder was lost. The utmost narrowing of the space is also signified by the tiny clearing where Alacindruska, the hyacinth flower, grows: "It was just as big as to fit a jug, with its mouth to the ground" (N. Tóth 1999, 7). Suffocating under the jug, Alacindruska can be the symbol of a minority forced into a dwindling space. Freeing her and letting her fine fragrance spread becomes parallel with a linguistic act, which makes the tale novel structurally complete. Alacindruska, who is freed from her tight space in the first chapter, saves her friends from the wavals and the antangels by shouting *ahay-hoo*, a Palots interjection, which is now used as a magic word. Thus Alacindruska offers the refuge of the language whereas Mányi, who resembles Moominmamma, provides the warmth of the hearth and the family and the nourishing cultural tradition.

5. Conclusion

The analysed examples suggest that representations of minorities in the Hungarian literature in Slovakia primarily emphasise uncomfortableness and oppressive confinement, whereas the alienating categories of externality and the insiderness inaccessible from outside are counterbalanced in the fairytale literature by the positive concepts of togetherness. Anikó N. Tóth's stories include the distressing tightness of minority space as part of the conflict of the tale and express the connection between space and identity and the identity losing functions of wandering and movement on an allegorical level. Analysing the tales from the aspect of multicultural theories shows that the relationship between space and identity in terms of being Hungarian in Slovakia can be most illuminated by raising awareness about the plasticity of the cultural background, the constructed nature of one's complete identity and the broader context of identity issues, instead of the frequently mentioned dichotomies such as mother tongue–second language, majority–minority nation, mother country–minority environment.

Grasping the questions of identity is supported by the polyphony of language variants. In this respect, linguistic diversity is represented not only by the layers of the Hungarian language in Slovakia or the dialects that can be utilised in literary texts, but also by the literary tradition that provides genres and linguistic patterns. Therefore, the writers' unique style variations are considered minor linguistic territories, and also the narrative elements which utilise genre patterns, which are the reflections of some collective experience or form of identity in code. The movements of the space confront us with movements of identity, and the spaces of minority also include the superimposition of different elements. The short prose of Pál Száz is an alloy of old

Hungarian and contemporary utterances, of the written and oral traditions; and the tales of Anikó N. Tóth are a combination of Palots linguistic elements, classic magic tales and allegorical stories. Such hybridity of a literary text results not only in the revaluation of typical motifs but also in the resituating of cultural knowledge.

List of references and sources

Balázs, Imre József. 2006. 'Minor és maior nyelvhasználati módok az erdélyi magyar irodalomban.' *Kissebségkutatás* 2. Accessed June 16, 2015. http://www.hhrf.org/kisebbsegkutatas/kk_2006_02/cikk.php?id=1368.

Boldizsár, Ildikó. 2012. *Meseterápia. Mesék a gyógyításban és a mindennapokban.* Budapest.

Chambers, Iain. 1994. *Migrancy, culture, identity.* London.

Deleuze, Gilles, and Félix Guattari. 1986. *Kafka. Toward a Minor Literature.* Translation by Dana Polan. Minneapolis.

Domokos Johanna. 2013. 'Mi a finn? Irodalom.' In *Finnek_! Multikulturális finn irodalmi olvasókönyv,* edited by Domokos Johanna, 39–60. Győr.

Drábeková, Zuzana. 2011. 'Podoby identity v dielach Tainaron Leeny Krohn a knihách o rodine Muminovcov Tove Jansson.' In *Veda pre vzdelanie – vzdelanie pre vedu II,* edited by Ondrej Mészáros, 37–42. Nitra.

— 2014. 'Kifelé a homokóra nyakából?' In *Trópusok, facebook, költészet,* edited by Zoltán Csehy, and Anikó Polgár, 215–222. Dunaszerdahely.

Grendel, Lajos. 1998. *Hazám, Abszurdisztán. Esszék és cikkek.* Pozsony.

Kirjuchina, Ljubow. 2000. *Sowjetdeutsche Lyrik (1941–1989) zu den Themen „Muttersprache" und „Heimat" als narrativers Identitätsakt.* Wiesbaden.

Koczur, László. 2003. 'Csipkerózsika – még mindig ébredőfélben.' In *Somorjai disputa (1). Az élő szlovákiai magyar írásbeliség c. szimpózium előadásai,* edited by Gábor Csanda, 75–103. Somorja.

Kozsár, Zsuzsanna. 2002. *Meseirodalmunk fája. A XX. század utolsó évtizedének szlovákiai* magyar prózai mesetermése. Pozsony.

Kümmerling, Bettina. 2003. 'Crosswriting und Mehrfachadressiertheit: Anmerkungen in der Kinderliteratur.' In *Am Rande bemerkt. Anmerkungspraktiken in literarischen Texten,* edited by Bernhard Metz, and Sabine Zubarik, 277–296. Berlin.

Martin, Holly E. 2011. *Writing Between Cultures. A Study of Hybrid Narratives in Ethnic Literature of the United Stated.* North Carolina.

Németh, Zoltán. 2005. *A bevégezhetetlen feladat. Bevezetés a „szlovákiai magyar" irodalom olvasásába.* Dunaszerdahely.

– 2013. 'A kisebbségi irodalom provokációja'. In *Kortárs magyar kisebbségi irodalmak. Posztkolonializmus, gender studies, littérature mineure,* edited by Balázs Imre József, 16–24. Kolozsvár.

N. Tóth, Anikó, and Ilona Németh. 1994. *Tamarindusz.* Dunaszerdahely.

N. Tóth, Anikó. 1999. *Alacindruska. Történetek Palóciából.* Pozsony.

Polgár, Anikó. 2011. 'The traditions of writing minority literary history.' In *Multilingualism and Multiculturalism in Finno-Ugric Literatures,* edited by Johanna Laakso and Johanna Domokos, 149–157. Wien.

Száz, Pál. 2017. *Fűje sarjad mezőknek. Phytolegendárium.* Pozsony.

Vida, Gergely. 2003. '„Nem vagyok önazonos". Gondolatok a nyolcvanas évek szlovákiai magyar költészetéről'. In *Somorjai disputa (1). Az élő szlovákiai magyar írásbeliség c. szimpózium előadásai,* edited by Gábor Csanda, 173–177. Somorja.

Writing in the dominant language

Eva Toulouze

1. Introduction

One of the problems one must often deal with when examining Finno-Ugric literatures is connected with the language used for writing these literatures. We have become accustomed to thinking about language as the first ethnic marker, and thus we automatically connect national literatures with the national language. However this has not always been the case in Russia's Finno-Ugric literatures. In this short overview I shall first discuss language identity in general and then its links with the beginning of a written culture among the peoples of Central Russia, analysing the kinds of literary work written in Russian that may still be categorised as belonging to the national literatures. Then I shall concentrate on more recent examples of the use of Russian by authors ethnically connected to the Finno-Ugric peoples of Central Russia. I shall conclude this overview by analysing the writings in Russian of authors belonging ethnically to the arctic peoples of Russia, the Khanty, Mansi and Nenets.

Language and identity have been thoroughly linked in the case of most of the Finno-Ugric peoples and languages, especially those who have acquired a symbolic model status, as with those of the three Finno-Ugric nation states – Hungary, Finland and Estonia. In their case there is no doubt that language is their first and the main identifier as ethnic groups and even as nations. *Nyelvében él a nemzet*[48] 'in its language lives the nation[49]', say the Hungarians, showing the connection as self-evident. In the 19th century, the Finns and the Estonians underwent multiple ethnic revival processes[50] that led to the development of an original written culture, of a language able to express the needs of contemporary social life, and finally to the creation of a State in 1919–1920. For them, language, as well as folk poetry, has been at the heart of their national movement. Within the same kind of process of ethnic revival, the ethnic groups in Russia, that asserted their rights and obtained political autonomy within the Soviet state in the 1920s and the 1930s (the Komi, the Udmurt, the Mari, and the Mordvinian), focused on language building: creating a literary language, teaching this language and writing in this language.[51] There is no doubt that all literary works created in these languages are part of these literatures. But what about works written in Russian, for example, by vernacular authors? Can we consider them part of these literatures? And what about the works of indigenous authors of the North, which are often written in Russian? And works by Sami writers written in Swedish, Norwegian, Finnish or Russian? Shall we consider Sergey Zavyalov a Mordvinian poet writing in Russian, or a Russian poet using Mordvinian themes? This last example is interesting because Zavyalov is a remarkable poet in Russian, who has influenced all of Russian contemporary poetry.

While the problem is interesting from a scientific point of view, it has very few practical consequences – for nothing prohibits us envisaging both approaches, which would probably be the most enriching way of studying their work. However here I am not interested in unravelling the influence of non-Russian authors on

48. This phrase is often assigned to István Széchenyi, but actually it has become a proverb.

49. 'Nation' taken as ethnicity. The political meaning of 'nation' as a set of citizens is not relevant in this part of the world, where under the influence of Herder's ideas, the word 'nation' has the meaning of a set of persons united by language, culture and what Herder called the "genius", a common spirit.

50. For the Finns it was at the beginning of the century, for the Estonians at the end of the same century.

51. Literature on these topics is abundant but scattered. Some useful general insights may be found in Lallukka 1990, as well as in Nanovfszky 2004.

Russian literature, but in the development of Finno-Ugric written cultures. Therefore I shall concentrate on the ethnic point of view, identify the phenomena we must analyse in the different regions, try to understand the possible reasons and motivations for a particular choice of language, and attempt to evaluate the possible impact.

Let us start chronologically. At the beginning of the literary history of the Finno-Ugric minority peoples are there any examples of works written in the dominant language, i.e. in Russian?

2. Early works of Finno-Ugric literature in Russian

There are indeed some examples of early works written in Russian, mainly in two particular genres, the memoir and epic poems. The first covers the decades immediately before and after the Revolution, while the second extends to the present period.

Actually, all Central Russia's Finno-Ugric ethnic groups in the last decades of the 19th and first of the 20th centuries had intellectuals able to write in their own tongue and in Russian. Most of them did not concentrate on writing artistic literature, but on other tasks aimed at developing a written culture: most Mari intellectuals dedicated their activities to preparing teaching materials – primers, textbooks, etc.; while Makar Evsev'ev, a Mordvin Erza author, published, in addition to numerous textbooks, the first ethnographic account of a *Mordvin Wedding* (1892). It has been subsequently published repeatedly. Ethnographic literature was thus also one of the genres written in Russian at the very beginning of the development of Finno-Ugric written languages, as in the case of Grigori Vereshchagin's monographs *The Udmurt of the Sosnovski Region* (1896) and *The Udmurt of the Sarapul uezd of the Vyatka Government* (1889). However, what I am mainly interested in here is the use of written forms to create art – literature in a more narrow meaning. Undoubtedly the two abovementioned genres correspond to this definition.

2.1 The Memoirs

The first genre is the memoir, and it touches particularly the Permian peoples, and on the Komi, Permyak and Udmurt. The works I refer to were mainly written before the Revolution, but the Permyak memoir was written in the 1920s in Finland. It is mainly in Permian literatures that we find the first memoirs written in Russian by Finno-Ugric authors. This concentration on Permian literatures is curious and I wonder why this phenomenon appears here and not in other regions. I have no outright answer to this question. Perhaps it has to do with the opportunities Udmurt, Komi and Komi Permyak authors had of gathering life experiences all around Russia and even abroad, which gave rise to the wish to share them with virtual readers, whereas the intellectuals of the Mari and the Mordvin were more bound to their region and did not wander as far away.

In the same years, at the beginning of the 20th century, a young Udmurt intellectual and a mature Komi scholar choose Russian to write autobiographical prose texts. Dmitri Korepanov, born in 1892 and better known under his pseudonym of Kedra Mitrey, writes as a twenty-year-old man about his experience as an indigenous student in missionary schools in a text called Дитя больного века[52] 'The Child of a Sick Century'. This manuscript was partly published in 1965. Its author had just been sacked from the Kazan seminary for teachers for indigenous schools because of a conflict about religion. At this point, Kedra Mitrey has not yet travelled as much as other authors, although he is far from home and moving around – even if it is only between his home village and Kazan – is a structuring aspect of his narrative since the emotions connected to it are often addressed in his literary work (cf. Dmitrieva 2014). Kedra Mitrey reports on his childhood and his life in his home village, on his conflict with his authoritarian father, and then on his studies and his relations with his teachers; eventually he is sacked and goes back to his family only to be thrown out by his father. He must then find his place in the world. The young man's emotions are at the centre of his dialogue with his reader. Researchers have discussed the genre of this text at length – the title given by Kedra Mitrey is "Short Novel", which implies a work of fiction, although the notion of journal and autobiography are also used –, as well as the artistic value it possesses, emphasising that it is the work of a beginner and that Korepanov was strongly influenced by contemporary

52. The published text is available at the following address: http://elibrary.unatlib.org.ru/pdfpreview/bitstream/handle/123456789/4807/invozho_05_09-28.pdf?sequence=1.

Russian memoir literature (Maratkanova 2007). Can we suppose that the existence of Russian models may have led to the choice of language? At the same time, while the church used vernacular languages in its practice and the young man had lessons in Udmurt at the seminary, we must not forget that his environment at the seminary was multi-ethnic and thus dominated by a common language, which was Russian. Moreover, it was not yet an common choice to write in Udmurt at the beginning of the 20th century. Udmurt had just begun to be used for literary aims: every year from 1906 an almanac in the vernacular had been published and these may be considered the first autonomous production in Udmurt[53] (cf. Istoriya I, 2004, 484). It is also should not be forgotten that the young man had literary ambitions, and these could at that time only be achieved in Russian.

53. The same kind of publication existed in Mari in the same years, after 1905. See as an example the Udmurt almanac of 2010 in its digitised copy handled by the Udmurt National library http://elibrary.unatlib.org.ru/pdfpreview/bitstream/handle/123456789/7655/knzh_pam_00051.pdf?sequence=3.

The Komi example is quite different. Its author, Kallistrat Zhakov, was born in 1866, so he was a bit younger than 50 when he writes his memoirs. He is a recognised intellectual, a professor at the Institute of Psycho-neurology in Saint-Petersburg. He also has a rich and controversial life experience – with a teacher's training he attempts to study forestry and maths, works for one year as a simple labourer, and lives in Kiev and Vologda (before moving, in later years, to Tartu and Riga), as well as developing a reputation as a philosopher.[54] His long prose text was published in four installations from 1912 to 1914 and then republished in 1996. Kallistrat Zhakov was a Komi, and a Komi activist, who endeavoured to keep in touch with his home region, where he conducted extensive fieldwork. But while he promoted his native language in his articles in the local press, his whole academic practice and writing was in Russian. Although there has been much more written in Komi before the Revolution, it was not an ordinary choice to write in a language that was not yet standardised.

54. About Zhakov: publications have become more frequent in recent decades after he was, for the most part, ignored during the Soviet period. On his heritage as a philosopher, see Zherebtsov and Miftahova 2010; more recently, Fadeeva 2015; Sozina 2015; Kuznetsova 2015; Lomonosova 2015.

The third example is even more marginal than these two. Ignati Moshegov (1880–1965) was only one decade older than Kedra Mitrey (cf. Istomin 2005). But he failed to fully live the Soviet experience of cultural construction: In the 1920s he emigrated through Estonia to Finland, where he published his autobiography "In the Eastern Devil's Cauldron" (В восточном чёртовом котле) in 1924. Here the choice of the language is dictated by the circumstances: the book was not intended to address Permyak readers, who were far away and unreachable, but a closer audience he could only touch through Russian.

2.2 Epic poems and epics

The second field in which we have Russian language literary texts in the Udmurt and Komi literary tradition is a very sensitive one.

Since the publication of the *Kalevala* (1835 and 1848), epics have had a particular meaning for the identity not only of Finno-Ugric peoples, but also peoples all around Europe. Actually, Finnish identity was built on the epic tradition of the Finnish people, which had been collected by Elias Lönnrot and other researchers and which provided the almost stateless[55] Finns both a history and a reputation as a people of bards, and thus the right to have a place among the civilised nations. The Estonians followed when Kreutzwald built up the Estonian epic, the *Kalevipoeg*, based on a similar, but not identical, tradition as the *Kalevala* – for poetic epic is unknown in the Estonian tradition, so Kreutzwald had to put legends and stories that circulated among the Estonian peasants into poetic form.

55. While the Finns were politically stateless at the international level, the Grand-Duchy of Finland had a fairly autonomous status within the Russian Empire.

Both the presence or absence of an epic tradition and, particularly, the existence and/or the creation of literary epics, are thus of major importance in the identity building experience of minority peoples. It is not surprising that writers and intellectuals endeavoured to give their peoples an epic.

The first attempts are from the same period as the memoirs and involve the very same authors the same year, 1916: Kedra Mitrey and Kallistrat Zhakov. They are both far from their homeland – Kedra Mitrey was in the Far East, in Blagoveshchensk, and Zhakov was in Saint-Petersburg. They turn to the epic traditions of their people and they do it in Russian.

While Kedra Mitrey was in the Far East, he wrote the first versified tragedy about an Udmurt folklore theme, *Esh Terek*, which is one of the first published books of Udmurt literature, although it is written in Russian. Nevertheless, the theme is undoubtedly Udmurt.

Curiously, although Esh-Terek is a hero and a leader of the Udmurt, it is not a heroic poem: Esh Terek is rather a romantic hero, who commits crimes and causes suffering to the Udmurt, and eventually acknowledges his faults and commits suicide. This theme will be later developed by another Udmurt writer (Nikolay Bayteryakov in 1975), this time in Udmurt.

In the same year, Kallistrat Zhakov writes a whole epic poem, referring to the old mythic state in the region that later will be the Komi or Permyak region, Byarmiya. The poem was written in 1916, but it was first published in its Latvian translation by Jan Rainis in 1924. The original, accompanied by a Komi translation, was published first in 1993.[56] Zhakov, as I mentioned, conducted extensive fieldwork in the Komi and Permyak regions. For the composition of his epics he used the stories he collected in the field, but also all his erudition about Scandinavian folklore and myths. For him, Byarmiya was not only a Komi, but also a Northern epic poem. It has been called the 'Komi Kalevala', but this name seems to be pretty exaggerated, when taking into account how precisely Lönnrot used the original poems collected from the bards. Even if Zhakov used some material he collected himself, he used ideas rather than texts. As a matter of fact, much of Byarmiya comes from his fantasy – a fantasy nourished by Komi folklore, but one with strong personal features.

56. The newest Russian edition is from 2013 (Zhakov 2013).

Zhakov's is not the only Finno-Ugric epic written in Russian in the first decades of the 20th century. The more brilliant figure in the Udmurt intellectual world of the 1920s, Kuzebay Gerd, had discovered the powerful influence of the *Kalevala* on Finnish identity (Kuznetsov 1994, 81) and he dreamt of doing what Lönnrot had done for the Udmurt. But in Udmurtia, the only epic songs known are those of the Dok'ja clan, with which Gerd was directly connected. We know that by around 1920 he had widely collected folklore with this aim (Jashin 1986, 86; Ermakov 1988, 207). Unfortunately, Gerd did not achieve his goal and all his materials disappeared in the storm that accompanied his elimination from the Udmurt public life and led to his execution in 1937. At the same time, he corresponded on this issue with a Russian ethnographer named Mikhail Khudyakov, who worked particularly on the Udmurt. On materials from Udmurt folklore, Mikhail Khudyakov actually wrote himself an Udmurt epic, dated 1920, although neither was this text published nor was its existence publically known. Khudyakov himself was executed some weeks after Gerd. In 1968 an Udmurt folklorist discovered the text in a library in Leningrad (cf. Bogomolova 1981, 14–15). It was published in 1976 with substantial cuts, and in the following decades not one but two Udmurt translations were achieved by V. Vanyushev (2008) and V. Shibanov (2008). This epic, although written by a Russian author, has been enthusiastically adopted by the Udmurt.

Somehow later, in 1933, another 'national' epic was published in Novosibirsk, a Mansi epic called *Yangal Maa*, by the Russian author Mikhail Plotnikov (1892–1953). While there are many indications in the lexical material that the story is also connected with other Northern peoples apart from the Mansi, clearly the material comes from the fantasy of the author, as well as Estonian scholar Aado Lintrop emphasises. Lintrop connects it more with Longfellow's "The Song of Hiawatha" than with the native epics of Finland or Estonia (Lintrop forthcoming).

3. Late works in Russian

In the last decades, one could have expected a renewal of the phenomenon. However, we must acknowledge that in spite of the regular decrease in Finno-Ugric language skills (as revealed by censuses since 1989[57]), in general we have not identified any trend to go over to Russian in the Udmurt, Komi and Mari literatures, or more precisely: we have not seen any rudiments of russified Udmurt, Komi and Mari occupying the literary space.

57. About Russian censuses, see Toulouze and Vallikivi 2016.

We have another example that fits well with the cases we commented on : in 2002 Anatoli Spiridonov, a writer and editor born in the Mari Republic, wrote the epic *Yugorno* in Russian, which is meant to be a Mari national epic. It is widely based on Mari folklore, has been translated into Mari and has been accepted by the Mari as their national epic (Koshaev 2015).

It is thus interesting to notice that such a sensitive field as national literary epics has been primarily occupied by Russian language texts, written either by indigenous writers (in the early pre-revolutionary period) or by Russian authors who, for one reason or another, have been interested in one particular nationality and have studied it in depth.

Among the Finno-Ugric peoples living in Central Russia, the Mordvinian are certainly the closest to the Russians and the most easily russified. They are spread over a huge territory, divided into two ethnic groups. This condition explains a spectacular decrease both in Mordvinian identity and in proficiency of language use over the two last decades: from more than a million (1,072,939) in 1989, according to the official Russian census, there were 843,350 Mordvinian in 2002 and 744,237 in 2010.

This explains that there is a significant part of the Mordvinian intelligentsia that uses Russian as a culture language. I will present two examples of intellectuals who write literature in Russian.

Vladimir Abramov comes from a very well known Erzya family: his father Kuzma Abramov (1914–2008) was a major Erzya writer who wrote mainly historical novels and developed powerful Erzya language prose. His son is a professor of history at Saransk University, but he has also asserted himself in the literary field, with an epic text written in Russian: "The Legend of the Silver Horseman"[58] was first published in 1996 and reached its fourth edition in 2015. The book has been awarded a Russian prize dedicated to Russian language writing. Based on Mordvinian mythology, this work follows the life of the mythical emperor Tyushtya.

58. In Russian: *Легенда о серебряном всаднике*.

The second intellectual I want to bring up is Sergey Zavyalov. He was born in Leningrad in a Mordvinian family and started publishing in samizdat. By refusing to use classic Russian verse and by adopting a rhythmic versification style, he soon made a name for himself in Russian poetry. He emigrated in 1994, lived some years in Finland and has now settled in Switzerland. While the Mordvinian inspiration is undoubtedly important in his writings, his historical contribution is clearly within Russian literary life[59], while he is pretty absent from the Mordvinian literary landscape.

59. As it appears clearly from his website http://www.vavilon.ru/texts/zavyalov0.html.

As a provisional conclusion, if we take into account the actual influence of the Russian-language writings, we may identify three groups of writers:

Those who write (at least some of their works) in Russian, but are of no relevance for Russian culture and literature. They are however important to the literary history of the people to whom they dedicated their writings, whatever their ethnic origin (e.g. Kedra Mitrey, Mikhail Khudyakov or Anatoli Spiridonov).

Secondly: Those who have a Finno-Ugric ethnic background and do not ignore it. They have (at least at the moment) succeeded in the difficult task of asserting their art within Russian literature and they probably will be remembered for bringing new themes and inspiration to Russian literature. Sergey Zavyalov is one of the authors who fall into this category.

Thirdly: Those who have succeeded in being present in both traditions. Historically we may mention Zhakov, who is considered one of the first Komi intellectuals and is so important for the Komi that immediately after having achieved a higher status of autonomy in the 1990s, the Komi organised his ashes to be brought back from Riga to Syktyvkar and raised a monument to him in Syktyvkar cemetery. At the same time, his poetry is highly regarded as innovative in Russian literary history.[60] We may conditionally set Vladimir Abramov into this category, although his work is too recent to assess whether and how long it will remain in the Russian literary tradition.

60. As emphasised by Russian scholar Yuri Orlitski in Syktyvkar, May 2016.

4. Hybridity

Hybridity has not been much represented in literary creation in Russia. The demographic and sociolinguistic situation has indeed led, in most regions, to the very heavy influence of Russian in everyday life and on the vernacular languages, whose use tends to be limited. When they speak their mother tongue, young people often use a mix of vernacular and Russian. A good and recent literary example in Udmurtia is a collection of poems that rapidly became very popular. It is characterised by the mix of Udmurt with lots of Russian. The author is Bogdan Anfinogenov (born 1990), who is a historian PhD student and also a renowned pop singer, better known as Ullapalla Boy on the stage. He is from a russified Udmurt family, but his knowledge of Udmurt has developed in the last years as he adopted the principles of ethnofuturism[61]

61. Ethnofuturism is an artistic trend developed by Estonian writers in the early 1990s, which emphasised avant-garde experiences rooted in folk tradition. It has been particularly successfully used in southern Estonia and by the Finno-Ugric peoples in Russia.

in his stage activity. He started writing poetry in Russian with a wide use of Udmurt words, and now writes in a hybrid kind of language that matches the way young people tend to use Udmurt, with some international words written in the Latin alphabet (mainly from pop culture). His collection of poems[62] elicited passionate reactions: a part of the younger generation was enthusiastic about it, while older Udmurt activists were utterly shocked. It received a literary Finno-Ugric award in Finland, which acknowledges the importance of this phenomenon.

62. In the original: *Айшет будущего*, Ижкар 2014.

5. The peoples of the North

I choose to set apart the peoples of the North – mainly the Khanty, the Mansi, and the Nenets – because their historical background is very different. Their connection to written culture is very recent and practically developed within the Soviet system, and because of this, in a rapid and voluntarist way (cf. Toulouze 1999). The Russian peoples of the North had not spontaneously developed a writing system for their languages, and in spite of serious attempts, evangelisation did not succeed in influencing the situation fundamentally. Soviet policy radically changed the situation: in 1925, a particular cycle of higher education was set in Leningrad in order to quickly train some intermediaries between the Soviet power and the indigenous peoples. These first students became the first linguists and writers, who helped create literary forms for their languages, to be taught in school and used to communicate with the population.

5.1 Early attempts

In the above mentioned period the task was huge: while these languages were poorly studied, the new intellectuals and their teachers had to identify for each language the different dialects, choose a dialect on which they would found the new literary language, establish orthography rules, describe the grammar … It took quite some time before the new languages were approved at an official linguistic conference in 1932. During this time, the teachers at the workers' faculty taught in Russian. The students in Leningrad published several issues of the University journal called "Taiga and Tundra". They wrote in Russian about their lives before and after the

Revolution (Eremeeva 2010). These are the first attempts to write literature in any of their languages.

The same approach was implemented in Naryan Mar, the capital of what would become the Nenets region, in 1930. The local literary journal decided to dedicate an issue to the young local Nenets writers and asked them to bring texts that were later heavily edited up to a level that allowed publication.

In this case, the 'choice' of language was not really a choice: first of all the texts were commissioned by official frameworks – school or journal. Secondly, there were actually no alternatives: the languages of the writers did not exist as literary languages, they were only oral communication tools.

But after the literary languages were approved and 'implemented' in school programmes, they were also used for literary creation: the first texts in Nenets were published between 1937 and 1940, and the first novel in Mansi in 1940.

5.2 Later experiences of writing in Russian

During the Soviet period, in different contexts depending on the period, the vernacular literatures of the peoples of the North existed, supported by State subsides. They did not produce immortal chef d'oeuvres, until the Mansi author Yuvan Shestalov appeared on the stage in the 1960s. Very quickly he became the emblematic Mansi writer, whose works were published in hundreds of thousands copies. While the first collection of poems was published in Mansi, very quickly Shestalov went over to writing in Russian. With *The Blue Winter of the Migration* (1964) he created a mix of prose and poetry. It is a text deeply rooted in Mansi tradition and mythology, similar to his Russian publications in the 1970s: *Pagan Poem* (1971), *When the Sun Cradled Me* (1972) and *The Secret of Sorni-Nay* (1976).[63]

63. About Shestalov, see Nagy 1997.

Shestalov's choices of language were supposedly influenced by the perspective of having thousands and thousands of readers. His successors probably had a different motivation, but Shestalov may have opened a door.

The three following authors are not marginal authors: they are the most representative and certainly the best of their people in the given period. They have written novels that will remain, which are as relevant as they are illuminating about the fate of those peoples, the Nenets and the Khanty. I shall present them in chronological order.

Anna Nerkagi (b. 1951) is a Nenets writer whose debut took place in 1977 with the novel *Anna from the Noho Clan* (see Samson Normand de Chambourg 1998). This is an autobiographical novel that tells the story of a Nenets girl who studies in town, is home sick, and yearns for the tundra. But when she goes home, she discovers that she isn't able to live there any more: she does not feel comfortable with the way of life, she cannot stand her father's smell. She doesn't belong any more: she yearns for the town. This important story, which for the first time is not tainted with propagandistic elements, is told in Russian, just like the author's subsequent prose texts. Anna Nerkagi is fluent in Nenets, and still she chose to write in Russian.

Actually, Nerkagi's route is not a simple one and her choices have often been contradictory: for a long time, she collected folklore in her language, while writing in Russian. Then she abandoned writing and dedicated herself to more practical tasks like setting up a *faktoriya*, a kind of exchange shop in the tundra. Then she turned towards Orthodoxy and founded a religious school for Nenets children and teenagers. Her relation with Russian is thus very close: she identifies herself as a go-between from one culture to the other.

Eremey Aipin (b. 1948) is an even clearer example. He is an Eastern Khanty prose writer who is fluent in his mother tongue, but was trained at the Gorki literary institute and writes almost exclusively in Russian. His first work, *Waiting for the First Snow* (1979), followed Anna Nerkagi's disturbing frankness: it expressed the perplexity of a young Khanty working in the oil fields while confronted with a worldview and behaviour so far from his own traditions. The following novel *In the Shade of the Old Cedar* (1981, 1986) is written in two languages. It was most probably written in Russian and translated into Eastern Khanty later. All of his following novels are written only in Russian: his epic novel, which sums up one century of the life of the Khanty, *The Khanty, or the Star of Dawn* (1990), has been translated into several languages, as well as his last novel published in Russian, *The Mother of God in Blood-red Snow* (2002), which is a tragic novel about the Khanty and Nenets uprising on the Kazym river in 1933–34. In between, he published *By a Dying Hearth* (1998), a poetic reminiscence of his childhood, which has so far only been translated into Hungarian.

So why have Nerkagi and Aipin preferred Russian over Nenets and Khanty to express themselves?

1. We should first turn to the subject of these works, which deal with issues that are vital to the Khanty and the Nenets. They all are concerned with relations between the native communities and the newcomers, the Russians. Clearly the authors' aims are not purely literary, i.e. artistic. Their addressee is not their community, which is totally aware of the problems denounced in these works, but the Russian intellectual community. The first goal of these novels is to raise awareness of what is going on in Siberia, and how the newcomers are destroying the indigenous cultures and communities, physically as well as spiritually. Another Khanty writer, Tatyana Moldanova, who is also an ethnographer, has written two short tragic novels in Russian, and gives another explanation of her language choice: she does not want to write depressing things in Khanty and therefore to a Khanty addressee. In Khanthy she would only write texts that would lift the Khanty's spirits, but she would denounce problems caused by the Russians in Russian.[64]

64. She declared as much at a meeting of Finno-Ugric writers in Syktyvkar in 1998.

2. Writing is not a traditional activity for the Siberian natives. It is not integrated into their way of life. It is an activity more connected with town dwelling. Aipin lives in cities and towns, while Nerkagi ceased any literary activity when she moved to the tundra. Cities and towns are heavily dominated by the Russian language. The decades that have passed since the approval of the literary languages have not allowed them to become deeply rooted in the use of the native

population. Especially since the 1960s native languages are no longer taught in schools, except at an elementary level, as foreign languages. Thus writing is an activity deeply rooted in the Russian world, and the Russian language is thus the natural tool of expression.

There is another writer who has been writing mainly in Russian: the poet Yuri Vella (1948–2013). His works are a mix of prose and poetry, mainly presented in a poetic form, except a collection of short stories, a short novel and three volumes of a Toponymical dictionary of the Agan River basin. Like Eremei Aipin, he studied at the Gorki institute, but much later, when he was almost 40 years old. His approach to languages in general is original: in his books he often added translations of his works into different languages. His vernacular language is Forest Nenets, a language for which no literary form has been elaborated. In 1990 he started a paper in Forest Nenets, creating a written language himself. After 8 issues he abandoned the project. This paper is called *TiLiwsama* 'Our Life' and Yuri Vella was the only writer. It contains short articles, poems, riddles, photos, etc., so it gave him good practice at Nenets writing. He also experimented with different kinds of poem. But he explains his choice of Russian as the literary language for most of his work with the peculiarity of his language, which is probably shared by other languages too. As he says, Forest Nenets is a language that functions in everyday communication (although not for everybody: in his region, no young people have been taught to speak Forest Nenets, while in other regions young people are proficient in spoken Forest Nenets) [65]. But even those who speak it have lost the artistic, metaphoric language of folklore and so are unable to use it anymore. In addition, writing poetry in the trivial language form that is used for speaking about money, work and everyday concerns does not seem proper.

65. See his website jurivella.ru for his works and studies about him.

6. Conclusion

In general there are two periods in which indigenous writers have been led to write in the dominant language: the first was at the beginning of the literary history of their people, when literary languages were not yet fixed and had not asserted themselves as an acceptable means of expressing oneself. This is true in the whole range of Finno-Ugric peoples, although the chronology is not always the same for all. During most of the Soviet era, vernacular languages dominated the literary landscape. Publishing in the vernacular was heavily subsidised by the state. We have no examples of native people writing in Russian. More precisely, none has written in Russian while remaining connected with the vernacular literatures – we cannot exclude the case of Russified writers of vernacular origins who made the choice to set these origins apart and to merge with the dominant nation.

In the last decades of the 20th century, the alternative to write in the dominant language emerges again for the peoples of the North, when their life is becoming increasingly endangered by the predatory exploitation of the natural resources of their habitat. They choose to denounce the degradation of their life conditions by addressing the people responsible for the depredations in their own language.

Moreover, at the beginning of the 21st century, a new postmodern phenomenon of hybridisation seems to be appearing in Central Russia, matching the influence of Russian on the vernacular languages.

Undoubtedly, most of these Russian-language texts are very deeply connected with the Finno-Ugric peoples, particularly because of the point of view of the themes dealt with. They become part of a wider dialogue, but as long as Russian-language texts are not turned towards external problems, which are not part of the native population's life, we cannot exclude them from their vernacular languages.

The cases of writers who have succeeded in entering Russian literature with their Russian language production is very rare. In the cases we have analysed, only one of them, Sergey Zavyalov, belongs in this category.

List of references and sources

Bogomolova, Zoja Alekseeva. 1981. Песня над Чепцой и Камой. Moscow.

Dmitrieva, Larisa. 2014. 'Преодоление локуса в повести Кедра Митрея' «Дитя Больного века», Филологические науки. Вопросы теории и практики: 58–60. Тамбов.

Eremeeva, O. N. 2010. «Институт Народов Севера в 1930: Первые шаги», Известия алтайского государственного университета, 2010-4, http://izvestia.asu.ru/2010/4-1/hist/TheNewsOfASU-2010-4-1-hist-16.pdf.

Ermakov, Foma K. 1988. Удмуртский поэт и писатель. Ижевск.

Fadeeva, Irina E. 2015. «Поэзия и философия Каллистрата Жакова как феномен русского модерна», Наследие 2: 7–16. Сыктывкар

Istomin, Fyodor. 2005. «Патриот без родины» Звезда. Accessed Octobre 25, 2005. http://zwezda.perm.ru/local/zvezda/page.php/zvezda/2005-10-25/4.

Istoriya I, 2004. История Удмуртии. Конец XV-начало XX века, Ижевск: УрО РАН, 2004.

Koshaev, Andrey V. 2015. «Марийский героический эпос Югорно: история создания, тематика, проблематика, поэзия», Огярёв online, Octobre 2015. http://journal.mrsu.ru/arts/marijskij-geroicheskij-epos-yugorno-istoriya-sozdaniya-tematika-problematika-poetika.

Kuznetsov, Nikolai S. 1994. Из мрака. Ижевск.

Kuznetsova, Tatiana L. 2015. «Творческое наследие К.Ф. Жакова и новейшая коми проза», Наследие 2: 34–51. Сыктывкар.

Lallukka, Seppo. 1990. *The East Finnic minorities in the Soviet Union.* Helsinki.

Lintrop, Aado (forthcoming). «Le poème Jangal-Maa et l'épopée mansie », Études finno-ougriennes 48. Paris.

Lomonosova, Marina V. 2015. «Каллистрат Жаков – профессор Невропсихологического института», *Наследие* 2: 52–65. Сыктывкар.

Maratkanova, Svetlana. 2007. Жанровое своеобразие повести Кедра Митрея «Дитя Больного века», Вестник Чувашского университета 3.

Nagy, Katalin. 1994. *Kellenek a szárnyák, míg tar taz út… (Juvan Sesztalov hatvan évés).* Budapest.

Nanovfszky, György. 2004, *The Finno-Ugric world.* Budapest.

Samson Normand de Chambourg, Dominique. 1998. *Ilir d'Anna Nerkagui: une page de vie autochtone dans le Grand Nord sibérien, 1917–1997.* Paris.

Sozina, Elena K. 2015. «Мифотворчество Каллистрата Жакова в контексте русского символизма», Наследие 2: 17–33. Сыктывкар.

Toulouze, Eva. 1999. «The Beginning of a Written Culture by the Uralic Peoples of the North», *Pro Ethnologia 6. Arctic Studies* 2: 52–85. Tartu. www.erm.ee/?node=160.

Toulouze, Eva, and Laur Vallikivi. 2016. «Les langues dans un miroir déformant», *Études finno-ougriennes* 47. Accessed november 30, 2016. http://efo.revues.org/4906.

Yashin, A. Daniyl. 1986. «Опыт создания удмуртского эпоса (о рукописи М.Г. Худякова Из народного эпоса вотяков)», Проблемы эпической традиции удмуртского фольклира и литературы: 82–98. Устинов.

Zhakov, Kallistrat F. 2013. Биармия, коми литературный эпос. Сыктывкар.

Zherebtsov, Igor L., and Miftahova, Olga R. 2010. «К.Ф. Жаков – Ученый, философ, пропагандист», Наследие 4. Сыктывкар.

List of contributors

Erika BENCE
Associate Professor
Department of Hungarian Studies
University of Novi Sad, Serbia
E-mail: erika.bence@ff.uns.ac.rs

Johanna DOMOKOS
Associate Professor
Institute of Arts Studies and General Humanities
Károli Gáspár University of the Reformed
Church, Hungary
Lecturer at Faculty of Lintugistics and Literary Studies
Bielefeld University
E-mail: domokos.johanna@kre.hu

Károly KÓKAI
Lecturer
Department of Finno-Ugric Studies

University of Vienna
E-mail: karoly.kokai@univie.ac.at

Johanna LAAKSO
Professor for Finno-Ugric Literature
University of Vienna, Institute for European and Comparative Linguistics and Literary Studies (EVSL)
Department for Finno-Ugristics
E-mail: johanna.laakso@univie.ac.at
Homepage: http://homepage.univie.ac.at/Johanna.Laakso/
Project ELDIA: http://www.eldia-project.org/
VIRSU network: http://www.univie.ac.at/virsu/

Enikő Molnár BODROGI
Associate Professor
Department of Hungarian Literature
Babeş-Bolyai University of Cluj-Napoca, Romania
E-mail: mbeniko@gmail.com

Vera Grigorievna PANTELEEVA
Candidate of Philology, Associate Professor,
Research Institute of National Education, Russia
E-mail: panvera@inbox.ru

Anikó POLGÁR
Associate Professor for Translation Theory and Hungarian Literary History
Department of Hungarian Language and Literature
Comenius University in Bratislava, Slovakia
E-mail: aniko.polgar@uniba.sk

Eva TOULOUZE
Professor of Finno-Ugric studies at INALCO, Paris
Researcher at Tartu University, Department of Ethnology
E-mail: evatoulouze@gmail.com

Finno-Ugrian Studies in Austria

Schriftenreihe für die Forschungsbereiche der Abteilung Finno-Ugristik (Institut für Europäische und Vergleichende Sprach- und Literaturwissenschaft) an der Universität Wien

Ao. Univ.-Prof. Dr. Andrea Seidler und Ao. Prof. Dr. Johanna Laakso

Johanna Laakso; Johanna Domokos (Eds.)

Multilingualism and Multiculturalism in Finno-Ugric Literatures

Multilingualism and multiculturalism are notoriously elusive concepts resting on partly controversial grounds. All too often diversity is defined by "othering" certain groups, emphasising their different or "exotic" characteristics. However, the diversity and dynamics of Uralic (Finno-Ugric) literatures deserve to be explored from the point of view of the interaction of multiple cultural and linguistic systems, structures and networks. With this volume, we want to invite all interested readers and researchers to consider the potential of Uralic literary multi–culturality in its entirety.

Bd. 8, 2012, 176 S., 19,90 €, br., ISBN 978-3-643-90162-0

Ágoston Zénó Bernád; Márta Csire; Andrea Seidler (Hg./Eds.)

On the Road – Zwischen Kulturen unterwegs

Dieses Buch beschäftigt sich mit kulturellen Kontakten zwischen dem ungarisch-, und deutschsprachigen Raum von den Anfängen im 14. Jahrhundert bis zur Gegenwart. Die Beiträge sind interdisziplinär, vorrangig aber kultur- und literaturwissenschaftlich ausgerichtet.

Es handelt sich um die erste Publikation, die die Frage des Kulturtransfers speziell für diesen Raum umfassend thematisiert.

Jelen kötet a magyar és a német nyelvterület közötti kulturális kapcsolatokkal foglalkozik a kezdektektol (14. század) egészen napjainkig. Bár a kötetben található tanulmányok interdiszciplináris jelleguek, elsosorban mégis a kultúra- és az irodalomtudományi kutatásokhoz kapcsolódnak.

Ez az elso olyan kiadvány, amely erre a térségre vonatkozóan átfogóan tárgyalja a kultúraközvetítés különbözo aspektusait.

Bd. 7, 2009, 360 S., 39,90 €, br., ISBN 978-3-643-50062-5

LIT Verlag Berlin – Münster – Wien – Zürich – London

Auslieferung Deutschland / Österreich / Schweiz: siehe Impressumsseite

Johanna Laakso (Hg.)

Ungarischunterricht in Österreich – Teaching Hungarian in Austria

Perspektiven und Vergleichspunkte – Perspectives and Points of Comparison

The Department of Finno-Ugric Studies at the University of Vienna is the only university institute in Austria where Hungarology is taught and the only institution outside the Hungarian-speaking area where teachers of Hungarian are educated. The problems of teaching Hungarian in Vienna, however, are not unique; for this reason, this collection of symposium proceedings includes contributions not only by experts of Hungarian language teaching but also by other professionals of applied linguistics, non-Indo-European and minority languages.

Bd. 6, 2008, 232 S., 19,90 €, br., ISBN 978-3-8258-1338-3

Johanna Laakso (Hg./Ed.)

Frau und Nation

Woman and Nation

The year 2006 marked the centenary of the Finnish parliamentary reform, in which the Finnish women as the first in Europe were acknowledged as citizens with full political rights. In this volume, researchers of history, linguistics and literature explore the diverse connections between gender roles and nation building, ethnicity, language, culture and identity in Northern, Eastern and Central Europe.

Bd. 5, 2008, 200 S., 19,90 €, br., ISBN 978-3-8258-1337-6

Norbert Bachleitner; Andrea Seidler (Hg.)

Zur Medialisierung gesellschaftlicher Kommunikation in Österreich und Ungarn

Studien zur Presse im 18. und 19. Jahrhundert

Bislang wurde noch nie versucht, die österreichische und ungarische Pressegeschichte in ihren Zusammenhängen und Überschneidungen (Redakteure, Journalisten, Verlage, Publikum) darzustellen. Die Vielfalt der Funktionen der Presse wird an Beispielen vorgeführt. Sie reichen von der Literaturvermittlung und Kommunikation unter den Gelehrten über pädagogische Fragestellungen und Akkulturation der Leser, Anzeigen für Buchhändler und das Lesepublikum bis hin zur Werbung für diverse Waren. Die Autoren des bewußt interdisziplinären Bandes sind ausgewiesene Fachleute auf dem Gebiet der Presseforschung und stammen aus Siebenbürgen, Österreich und Ungarn.

Bd. 4, 2007, 304 S., 34,90 €, br., ISBN 978-3-8258-0500-5

Johanna Laakso

Our Otherness

Finno-Ugrian Approaches to Women's Studies, or vice versa

"Our Otherness" explores the interface between Finno-Ugrian Studies – traditional research into the Finno-Ugric languages, their history and relatedness, as well as other approaches to the language, history, culture, and folklore of these peoples – and Women's Studies. How do gender and linguistic origins interact in the making of national identity? Can we speak about a "gendered Finno-Ugrianness"? How does gender express itself in languages lacking grammatical gender, and how are these questions dealt with in language description and language planning?

Bd. 2, 2005, 200 S., 19,90 €, br., ISBN 3-8258-8626-3

Katalin Blaskó; Timothy Riese

Übungsgrammatik Ungarisch

Mit der Übungsgrammatik Ungarisch erscheint zum ersten Mal ein groß angelegtes Werk, das Ungarischlernenden die Möglichkeit bietet, die mannigfalte und manchmal verwirrende Formenlehre des Ungarischen gründlich zu erlernen und zu üben. Das Buch wendet sich an alle, die sich schon elementare Kenntnisse in Grammatik und Wortschatz angeeignet haben. Die Formenlehre wird systematisch und detailliert dargestellt, nach jedem Punkt stehen Übungen, die der Einprägung des Gelernten dienen. Das Buch eignet sich zum Selbststudium (Schlüssel zu den Übungen enthalten), als Kurslehrbuch und als Nachschlagewerk.

Bd. 1, 2018, 792 S., 39,90 €, br., ISBN 978-3-8258-8624-0

LIT Verlag Berlin – Münster – Wien – Zürich – London

Auslieferung Deutschland / Österreich / Schweiz: siehe Impressumsseite